Are You Saved?

"Examine yourselves, whether ye be in the faith..."

Preface

Preliminary Discourse

Chapters:

Preface

There is no need for me to give a testimony from myself in this preface, or in this book at all unless it pertains directly to the discussion at hand. I'll not spend much time carrying on about what the Lord has done for me, or what I wish He would do for me now. He has already done more for me than I could ever comprehend. How could a perfect God, holy and just in all His ways, not only let me continue existing in this wretched life, but knowing who I was and what I would do, send His only Son to die in my place to be the propitiation for my sin-debt to the law as a vile and wicked sinner? That is where I am hung up. That is where I come undone. That is where my mind will dwell for the rest of my days. I cannot grasp what was done for me on that cross.

I am not impressed with the pseudo-holiness of the charismatics. I am not impressed at the impetuous use of tongues. I am not even impressed at the thought of a man being raised from the dead, or cancer disappearing from the body. I am much like a mouse locked in the jaws and coils of a serpent. I am stuck at this. I cannot get past the finished work of God through His Son Jesus Christ at Calvary. What was done on that cross is incomprehensible. It is simple enough that a child can understand, yet deep and wide enough that not even the most noble and educated expositor can sound its depths.

Many educated expositors of Scripture can carry a sense of pride in their education. Though we know that is sinful, we have to be careful not to fall off the other side of that line. People who hold a negative attitude towards the educated ones for simply being educated fall into pride on the other side of the line. They have pride in not being educated. They feel some need to exclaim that they do not have an education, and the ones that do are in some kind of error by striving to get "letters" behind their name. By the grace of God, I am not in either one of those categories. If a man is not careful, the more liberal leaning Bible Colleges and Seminaries can sway them into heresy by teaching them that it is ok to teach or preach in a fashion that doesn't bring out the blade of Scripture. On the other side of the line, a non-educated wild man can come out of the gate swinging a bat of truth with no balance of grace and really do more damage than good. The heavy grace approach will make a man comfortable in his sin and will ultimately lead to damnation. The heavy truth approach will make salvation seem unattainable and the hearer will soon cease from the faith, knowing they can never live up to the standards set forth by the speaker. That also will ultimately lead to damnation.

There is a blade's edge on which one must walk to remain both in truth and in grace. It requires much discernment, much prayer, much fasting, and much time in the Word of God. I will not pretend that I am tiptoeing perfectly center in the truth and grace spectrum. Even though I am striving to do so, everyone bears some measure of error in their ways. As of now, I am a layman from rural southern Mississippi. I am an "uneducated" man on paper, but being immersed in the Word of God and consistently surrounded by other godly men (who are educated) have proven to be sufficient means in my growth in grace. As grace would have it, that is all that the Bible suggests we need. God, His Word, and gathering with other believers. Whether I am led to change my formal education status in the future or not, I am content knowing that I am in the providence of the perfect God who will direct my paths according to His will.

Preliminary Discourse

Of all the theological questions that float around the different denominational circles of Christendom, there is a lot of subject matter that could be up for debate. We could discuss the different viewpoints of eschatology (which seems to be the most "exciting" topic in today's society) and where we stand personally on this topic. There are several major stances one could take here, which include: The "preterists", the "partial preterists", and the "futurists". The term "preterist" comes from the Latin word *praeter,* which simply means "past". Full preterists hold that all things concerning eschatology, or the "end of things", have already come to pass. Futurists hold that all things concerning eschatology have yet to come to pass. And, as you have probably already discerned, the partial preterists land somewhere in the middle. These are not the only areas for eschatological discussion. You still have all of the "millers" to deal with. You know; the pre-mills, the post-mills, and the a-mills. I'm sometimes impressed at how we can all read the same Bible and come up with so many different viewpoints, but here we are. Isn't it exciting?!

We could also discuss and debate other secondary items, such as the most accurate translation of Scripture. No matter where you stand on this particular subject, be sure of this: Someone out there disagrees with you and is willing to fight over it! The two most common categories that people fall into here are "King James Only", and "Hey, just give me an English translation!" I personally prefer the King James version to read and study, but I am not of the opinion that the King James Version is the ONLY accurate translation. I regularly look at the original languages and do "word studies", and I often look at modern translations to see how they have translated a verse and which English words they used compared to the KJV in some instances. Proverbs 11:14 says that *"in the multitude of counselors, there is safety"*, and I believe the wisdom in that passage applies to everyone in almost any area of life. Some may not agree with me in this since so many translations read differently (and some a lot differently), but I consider it a blessing that I can see three or four different ways to say the same thing. Some translations are more "word for word" while others are more "thought for thought". In my opinion, it doesn't dilute the message to have a few solid and accurate translations to pull from. If anything, it helps strengthen my understanding.

Many of the arguments set forth by "King James only" advocates fall apart at the seams in my opinion, but I love and respect all of them. Some would say that it is the only true Word of God. To those I would humbly ask, should all French, Russian, Japanese, and other non-English speakers have to learn an archaic dialect of English to even be able to read and/or hear about the Savior? It is a beautiful translation (and it's my favorite), but if it's the ONLY true Word of God, the seventy-five percent of the world that does not speak English is in big trouble. To add further, English wasn't even a language until four or five hundred years after Christ walked the earth, and even then, those early dialects of "English" wouldn't be recognizable by us today.

For these simple reasons, I can't stand with the KJV only crowd on this matter. But to go a little further, what did the church use for the first ~1600 years of its existence if they didn't have the true Word of God? What makes English speakers so special? Then some others may say, "Well, it was the standard for 400 years!" Going by that logic, I would say that the Latin Vulgate was the standard for over 1100 years. So, there's that… Even with these disagreements, it is a blessing that this is a topic that we can disagree on and still truly defer to one another as brothers and sisters in Christ. I am partial to the King James Version and I believe it still deserves to be read and used today, but if you read an ESV or NASB, I will not think less of you. I would much rather someone have an NIV that reads it, than to have a KJV that lives on a shelf!

What about our opinions on worship in general? Is there not plenty of subject matter there that could be up for debate? There are two major camps here also, and you the reader can discern which side you are on. There are those that hold to the normative principle of worship and those that hold to the regulative principle of worship. Let me break those two stances down briefly if you're not familiar: Those that hold to the *normative* principle of worship believe that anything is permissible in worship as long as the Bible doesn't explicitly prohibit it. On the other hand, those that hold to the *regulative* principle of worship believe that only the things put forth in Scripture concerning worship are permissible. I personally tend heavily to the latter. It may seem innocent to use a smoke machine and a light show to "intensify" the worship service, but remember this; If you use worldly means to draw a crowd, you will need worldly means to keep a crowd. If you want to really see what you have, simply turn the regular lights on, sing from the hymnal, and preach chronological expository sermons from the Bible week after week for a year. If you need someone to put on a show for the worship to be good enough for you to attend, I would ask, "Whose worship are you interested in, yours or His?"

As you can see, there is much room for debate on many different topics in Christendom. But there is one ringing question that, without a doubt, has gone through the minds of most people that have ever professed Christ as Lord and Savior. "Am I saved?" Some may say that it is not good to doubt, but Paul called the souls in Corinth to examine themselves. I also call you the reader to examine yourself to see if you are in the faith! (*2 Cor. 13:5*) I have almost 40 years of life behind me at this time, and most of that has been spent attending a local church on a weekly basis. Sadly, I can count on one hand how many times I have been asked if I was saved. I have been addressed with the crowd from a pulpit to examine myself, but almost never directly. I suppose the ministers assumed that since I kept coming back, I was upright and didn't need any special attention other than the general exhortation from the pulpit.

Here in the deep south, we have a lot of "good ole boys" that believe that since they go to the church services, they are saved. They may get their comfort from being in the "good graces" of everyone at the local church, or from sharing Christian-type posts on social media. They may feel secure because they walked the aisle as young teens and were baptized. They may have a false sense of security because their parents and grandparents are buried behind the church, or that their parents are good people, not knowing that they are, at this very moment, dancing over the roof of Hell - and make no mistake, that roof is weak and fragile! At any moment, God could drop His hand of mercy and they would fall into everlasting torment. I myself lived in that state for over a decade. I was not saved, though I thought I was…

In this writing, I have two goals and both are for a single purpose. By the Scriptures, I would like to help offer some readers the comfort and assurance of their salvation, if indeed they have been born again. I would also like to make it clear to the ones who are reprobate, and "playing church" like I was, that they should have no assurance of salvation and except they repent with Godly sorrow, they will end up separated from anything good that God has for them, forever. All for this single purpose; for the glory of God.

I would like to take the first two chapters of this book and let Scripture make the "great divide" between itself and other religions. For you to know if you are saved or not, you must first know what the Bible says about *why* and *how* we are saved. As for the *"why"*, it is for the glory of God. He saves wretched sinners for His own glory. He saves wicked men so that when a change is wrought in a life for everyone to see, the world would speak of Him and what He has done. We are really good at making everything *about us*. While we are the magnificent beneficiaries of His redeeming work, everything He does is for His own glory, not ours. The first two chapters, though not exhaustively, will hopefully lend somewhat of a helping hand in explaining the *"how."*

The following chapters will be focused on sifting through the Word of God to find the distinguishing characteristics of what a saved soul looks like, and what a lost soul looks like to help the reader answer the burning question that we have all asked ourselves, "Am I saved?" Chapters 3-10 will be dedicated to helping the reader determine for themselves the answer to that question. Chapter 11 will be the discussion on the value of the Scriptures themselves and what they should mean to the one who professes Christ as Lord and Savior. Finally, the book will close with a pure and accurate explanation of the Gospel of Jesus Christ. *"For I am not ashamed of the gospel of Christ: for it is the power of God unto salvation to every one that believeth..."* (Romans 1:16)

1

By Faith Alone

The entirety of this book revolves around a single and solemn command given by the Apostle Paul: *"Examine yourselves, whether ye be in the faith; prove your own selves."* (2 Corinthians 13:5) This is not a casual suggestion, but a spiritual mandate. In an age saturated with outward religious activity, we are commanded by Scripture to look *inward*, which I can assure you is harder than any other place to look! We have to stop merely assuming the answer and prove it by the only reliable metric- the Word of God.

I grew up in an era of error, and I'm afraid those times are still among us. I walked an aisle when I was a young teen (late 1990s). I did what I was told that I had to do to be saved. I said "yes" to the series of questions asked of me and I was immediately turned around and presented before the congregation as one that had "made Jesus the Lord of his life." There was no further discussion of faith. There was no further discussion of repentance. There was no further discipleship (aside from the normal Sunday and mid-week services). Simply a baptism the following week, and that was it…

Moving on in life, as a late teen, my true colors began to show. I was just like countless others that took that walk. I was living for the world in most aspects of life. I knew how to "play the part" in front of others. I would work myself to the bone, helping people, volunteering at our local fire department, and other things that would make anyone think that I was upright. And, according to man's standard, I was. By my own definition I was a "good ole boy." I had the respect of the old folks in the community because I was polite (in front of them) and a hard worker. But how did I act when none of those old men were watching me? How did I act when it was just us "boys"? To condense it down into one sentence: Those older folks would have lost respect for me.

I knew what the Bible said about sin, but I was as cold as a stone to it all. I warmed the pew almost every week, but none of my peers that *really* knew me or knew how I was called me out for leading a life of sin. Could it be that they were living the same lie that I was living? I thought I was saved because I said that I "believed." But my younger self's faith was rooted and grounded in my own ability to walk an aisle and say "yes" when I was supposed to say "yes." My faith was in my own profession of faith, as odd as that may sound... Yet, the core of who I was remained unchanged. I was a product of what I later found to be known as "decisional regeneration." My conscience was not pricked. I didn't possess the characteristics of a believer. I even thought that I was sorry for my sin, but it was not godly sorrow that led to repentance. It was worldly sorrow, which leads only to death. (2 Corinthians 7:9-10) I was like a criminal who was sorry only because he got caught, but not because my conscience was troubled during the acts of rebellion against God.

Does this sound anything like you, or am I alone? If you are reading this book, you either have questioned, or are questioning your salvation. To answer that question, we must first properly define the element that grants salvation, which is faith. According to Hebrews chapter eleven, faith is the unbroken theme and the identifying characteristic of all of God's people. The writer of Hebrews gives us the foundational definition in chapter eleven. *"Now faith is the substance of things hoped for, the evidence of things not seen."* (Hebrews 11:1) If we examine the Greek term (*hupostasis*) translated as "substance," we find that same word is translated in other places as "confidence" or "confident." That being said, faith is literally the confidence you have in things hoped for but cannot see. Some of the more modern translations use the English word "assurance."

I often use this simple analogy when trying to describe faith: Think about the last time you simply sat down at a dinner table. In the moment that you sat down, you didn't have to consider whether or not the chair that you sat in would hold you. Without a moment of hesitation, you put your complete and unwavering faith in that chair and sat down. You had such assurance that the chair would hold you, the thought of it failing never crossed your mind. But what about saving faith?

We know that Hebrews 11:6 says, *"But without faith it is impossible to please him: for he that cometh to God must believe that he is, and that he is a rewarder of them that diligently seek him."* How can we be sure our faith is a *saving* faith, and not a menial, unworthy faith? Is it possible to know about God and remain lost? The only way to truly answer that is to turn to the absolute Truth for clarity. *"Thou believest that there is one God; thou doest well: the devils also believe, and tremble."* (James 2:19) I conclude that, according to this particular passage, it is possible to believe with your mind, but your heart be left unchanged. If you think this thing out, you'll realize sooner or later that the *devils* know more truth about who God is than we do. They were created by Him and once dwelt with Him in paradise, and now tremble at the mention of Him who is sovereign over all! The big word for this is *"intellectual assent"*, but it's not saving faith. It is knowledge without commitment, fact without trust, meat without butter… You get the idea.

Furthermore, in the Gospel of John, we see that even witnessing Christ's miracles is not enough! *"Now when he was in Jerusalem at the passover, in the feast day, many believed in his name, when they saw the miracles which he did. But Jesus did not commit himself unto them, because he knew all men, and needed not that any should testify of man: for <u>he knew what was in man</u>."* (John 2:23-25) We can now surely conclude that not only can you *know* with your mind, but you can also *see with your own eyes* Christ Himself performing miracles and remain lost and without saving faith.

Saving faith is not a mere cognitive recognition of certain facts, but it is a gift of God that leads to a total reliance *on*, and resting *in*, Christ alone. It is the full assurance that your own merits are worthless and that only His finished work is sufficient. *"For by grace are ye saved through faith; and that not of yourselves: it is the gift of God: Not of works, lest any man should boast."* (Ephesians 2:8-9)

"Knowing that a man is not justified by the works of the law, but by the faith of Jesus Christ, even we have believed in Jesus Christ, that we might be justified by the faith of Christ, and not by the works of the law: for by the works of the law shall no flesh be justified." (Galatians 2:16)

Salvation can only be by faith and faith alone in the Son of God, the Lord Jesus Christ. He is the rock upon which we stand. Let no man convince you that salvation is by any other means.

Even though you may feel like you need to "do something" to prove yourself to God and men, rest assured that this is a trap that MANY fall victim to. Do you not know that He can discern the intent of your actions, and even your thoughts? *"For the word of God is quick, and powerful, and sharper than any twoedged sword, piercing even to the dividing asunder of soul and spirit, and of the joints and marrow, and is a discerner of the thoughts and intents of the heart."* (Hebrews 4:12) Make no mistake about it; you can put on a fantastic outward show to fool a man, but you cannot fool God!

Since salvation is *by faith alone in Christ alone*, how do you get this faith? And since true faith is a gift, what evidence does it produce in the heart and life of the one who receives it? Yes, real evidence! As the rest of this book unfolds, we will look at the Scriptures and plainly see internal and external marks that prove whether your faith is genuine and that you are on the narrow road *"to an inheritance, incorruptible and undefiled."* (1 Peter 1:4), or if you are on the broad road that leads to *"outer darkness, weeping, and gnashing of teeth."* (Matthew 8:12)

2

Not by the Deeds of the Law

The major dividing line between Christianity and all other religions of the world is this: Works! Every other spiritual system that I know of, from the most ancient to the most modern, dictates a set of deeds, rituals, or at least, observances required to placate, impress, or achieve reconciliation with the divine creator. The standard is pretty much universal and it goes something like this: "You messed up. You must *do this or that* to be made right." Christianity stands alone with this radical, singular declaration: You are saved by the finished work of Christ alone, through faith alone, apart from the deeds of the Law.

Sadly, this plain foundational truth has always been a topic of confusion and debate among Christians. There are some circles of Christianity that are returning again to the Old Testament dietary laws, thinking that somehow, they might be more pleasing to God by striving to follow them. They may say, "I believe that salvation is by faith alone in Christ alone, *but* I also want to wear this *yoke of bondage* around my neck to hopefully be more pleasing to God."

In doing so, they are subconsciously finding peace and assurance in their own ability to "do something" instead of resting completely in the work that has already been accomplished. This is almost precisely the error the Apostle Paul fought in the churches of Galatia in the first century! (This isn't anything new...) Back then, Judaizers were convincing the Galatians that they had to be circumcised and adhere to Jewish rules and traditions to be saved. In other words, they were adding something to Christ's finished work. And to be honest, I can see where the confusion came from back then, just as I can see where the confusion with the Torah-observant crowd comes from today. In the first century, they were confused over circumcision, which is an Old Testament law. That's exactly what the Torah observers are doing today by trying to add back the Old Testament dietary laws. Nevertheless, in a fiery letter from Paul, they were boldly rebuked for adding ANYTHING to the Gospel of Jesus Christ! He went so far as to call it *"another gospel"* (Galatians 1:6). Paul made their error very clear, time and time again: *"I do not frustrate the grace of God: for if righteousness come by the law, then Christ is dead in vain."* (Galatians 2:21)

This is a sobering conclusion that should clear up any muddy water. Adding any human work to the Gospel is grave error. Whether it's keeping dietary laws, performing ceremonies, or simply being a "good person" to try to earn salvation, at the end of the day, it is frustrating the grace of God and making the death of Christ to no effect. Why did Christ need to die if you could have earned righteousness by diligently adhering to the law? The answer is simply that He did not have to die if righteousness was attainable by our power and ability to adhere to the law! And by attempting to do so is a direct offense to the sufficiency of the cross. Furthermore, concerning the dietary laws while we're here, let me add that Jesus Himself said: *"Not that which goeth into the mouth defileth a man; but that which cometh out of the mouth, this defileth a man."* (Matthew 15:11) Because of that, I can say unashamedly that I prefer to eat shellfish with thin strips of salty pork wrapped around it! *Selah*

Some other groups of well-meaning Christians hold that outward works are required to be saved. We have to be very careful here, and I do not want anyone to take this lightly because it can be hard to navigate. Jesus himself gave dire warning against relying on outward activity in the most chilling and sobering passage (my opinion) in all of Scripture!

"Not every one that saith unto me, Lord, Lord, shall enter into the kingdom of heaven; but he that doeth the will of my Father which is in heaven. Many will say to me in that day, Lord, Lord, have we not prophesied in thy name? and in thy name have cast out devils? and in thy name done many wonderful works? And then will I profess unto them, I never knew you: depart from me, ye that work iniquity." (Matthew 7:21-23)

I want you to see what they professed on that great day of judgment. They appealed to their own works. They said, "I prophesied! I cast out devils! I did many wonderful works!" Not only that, but they emphatically declared Jesus as "Lord, Lord!" So, we see that good works are obviously not the answer.

Now, let's get a little more personal. What will you say on that great day if God were to ask, "Why should I let you in?" Will you begin rattling off your works like these poor souls did? Would you say, "Lord, I went to church every time the doors were open! I tried not to cuss too much, and I tithed every week! I stopped eating these certain foods, and I even stopped watching T.V.!"? The truth is, we all want to appeal back to our own works to show what we have done to earn something. It's almost like we have a factory setting of "Look what I did to earn *such and such*!" That is in simple terms called "pride", and it's hard to shake. It is vital that we remind ourselves daily that we have a sin-debt that we could not pay, but praise be to God Almighty that Holy justice cried out "SATISFIED" from that old rugged cross at Calvary! The sin debt has been PAID IN FULL for all of His people. But somehow, this still isn't "good enough" for some.

However, as you read through the Bible, you will notice some "speedbumps" that can cause us to think this way. But we must dig a little deeper on the things that we don't understand rather than taking them at face value or ignoring them altogether. When you encounter something that you don't agree with, or that doesn't make sense to you, consider it a blessing. A wise man once said that when we encounter truths in Scripture that we don't like or agree with, it can be a "springboard to sanctification." By digging in the Word and shaping our minds to truths that we find uncomfortable is an avenue to spiritual growth. One "speedbump" that we encounter concerning works is here: James *seems* to suggest something different in his epistle when he said, *"Was not Abraham our father justified by works, when he had offered Isaac his son upon the altar?... Ye see then how that by works a man is justified, and not by faith only. Likewise also was not Rahab the harlot justified by works... For as the body without the spirit is dead, so faith without works is dead also."* (James 2:21-26) This seems to stand in contrast to Paul's powerful statement in Romans 4. *"For if Abraham were justified by works, he hath whereof to glory; but not before God. For what saith the Scripture? Abraham believed God, and it was counted unto him for righteousness."* (Romans 4:2-3)

We have two places in Scripture that seemingly contradict each other if taken at face value. Paul mentions Abraham's justification *by faith* from Genesis 15. James mentions Abraham's justification *by works* from Genesis 22 (when he

9

offered Isaac upon the altar). The key to resolving this tension is the *audience* for the justification. Justification *before God* is what Paul wrote about in Romans 4. This is the moment a person is declared righteous by God through faith alone. This happened to Abraham in Genesis chapter 15. This is the means of salvation and having a right standing legally with God. Justification *before men* is what James wrote in his epistle. This is the moment a person proves that their faith is genuine in an outward manner to the world and to themselves. This happened to Abraham in Genesis 22. This is simply the evidence of salvation. Since Abraham was justified by faith in Genesis 15, he did not *need* to be justified again in Genesis 22. What we are seeing in James is an instance by which Abraham's internal, saving faith was able to be seen outwardly. As James also says, *"shew me thy faith without thy works, and I will shew thee my faith by my works."* (James 2:18)

This distinction is critical, but can often be confusing. Christians perform outward works *because they are saved.* Christians do not work *to be saved.* If you have no works, that could be a strong sign that you do not truly have saving faith, because faith without works is dead. But simply performing works does not guarantee you have come to saving faith (remember, Matthew 7:21-23).

Since salvation is not attainable by the deeds of the law or any work of your own, how does a person move from being "dead in sin" to possessing this "saving faith" that produces good works? This transition is accomplished by the supernatural work of God called *regeneration.* The natural man is spiritually dead and deaf to the Gospel, and held captive by a sin nature. Jesus said: *"No man can come to me, except the Father which hath sent me draw him."* (John 6:44) This drawing is God's *effectual call*, which is always successful. This is not a general, outward call of the Gospel that can be rejected, as if it were coming from a man. When the Spirit of God calls out to the heart of a sinner, He makes them spiritually alive! He *regenerates* them. This is being born again. This new birth is what immediately causes saving faith to spring up in the heart. This faith, in turn, produces the inevitable and visible fruits of good works, repentance, and a desire for holiness that the epistle of James seems to suggest should come from a saved soul. Salvation is a gift from beginning to end, and our works are merely the evidence that we have received it.

Hopefully, you are convinced (by Scripture, of course) that salvation is by faith and faith alone in the person and finished work of the Lord Jesus Christ. Now that we have established and made clear what saving faith is, what produces it, and what it produces, the next 8 chapters of this writing will be dedicated to looking at the distinguishing characteristics of the lost and of the saved as they are found in Scripture. This will be a worthy exercise in order to follow Paul's command to *"Examine yourselves, whether ye be in the faith..."*

3

A New Creature

"Therefore if any man be in Christ, he is a new creature: old things are passed away; behold, all things are become new." (2 Corinthians 5:17)

Throughout the next chapters, I will ask you to look in the mirror. This is obviously not meant to be a literal request for you to get up and go find a mirror, but it is simply asking you to look back on something that no one else can really see; the *real you*. It's a request for you to look back on your own life, and your own actions, and the motivating factor behind those actions.

In the passage mentioned above, it implies that if anyone is saved, they have become a new creature. But what exactly does that mean? It obviously doesn't mean that God changes us into a different type of animal. If He turned all saved humans into horses, there wouldn't be a need for me to write this book! It would be useless because THAT difference could be observed from a mile away! While it may sound silly, that is exactly what He does on the inside of a man when He justifies him! He does not change the outward appearance of the man, but He absolutely changes the heart! As prophesied, *"A new heart also will I give you, and a new spirit will I put within you: and I will take away the stony heart out of your flesh, and I will give you an heart of flesh."* (Ezekiel 36:26)

God told us exactly what He would do concerning the heart of a man through the prophet Ezekiel, and He is not slack concerning His promises! When the Great I AM declares a matter to be so, you can take it to the bank! Have you ever witnessed a vile and wicked sinner come to repentance and faith in Christ? They literally become a completely different person on the inside, which also manifests change on the outside. The further out into the world a person is before they come to faith in Christ, the more of a radical change you can see in them, even to the point that some upstanding church folks would call them "religious fanatics." It's like they are looking at the world through a different set of eyes, talking in the world with a different mouth, walking with different feet, thinking with a different mind, etc. Everything about them seems different! What else could we expect to see when God Himself takes out the heart of stone and gives to them a heart of flesh?

The stony heart is hard, cold, and unresponsive. It does not feel genuine conviction over sin. If anything, it only fears the consequences of being caught. The stony heart is proud and self-righteous, perfectly content to believe its own works are sufficient for God. It hears the Word of God like a hammer hitting rock. There's a loud noise but no impression is left and no change seems to take root. The heart of flesh, however, is softened so that it is tender and responsive. When the heart of flesh sins, it doesn't just feel remorse, or fear worldly consequences. It's much deeper than that. It feels grief for offending the God who loves it. It desires to be cleansed. It is broken and contrite, yet it is also alive and able to receive and obey the Spirit. This transformation from a heart of stone to a heart of flesh is what it means to be born again, or to be *regenerated.*

I don't want to get too much further into this discussion without getting a little more personal (or, as personal as I can get through written words). Can you see such a change in your own life? I'm not talking about "growing up," or simply becoming more mature as we age. Even the self-proclaimed atheist does that. I'm aiming at the heart. Is a change of heart evident in your life? At this point, you can take that first look into the mirror of your own life and examine yourself. Can you look back over the course of your life and see a change of heart? Can you look back on the person you once were and see a clear difference when you look at yourself today? Make no mistake, I am not talking about measuring your performance, or gauging your success by your own ability to walk circumspectly. That is part of it and we will discuss that in more detail later on, but for now I want to go deeper than that. Is your heart changed? You were once your own master; or in other words, *a slave to the world's dictates*. Now, your ultimate authority is Christ, expressed through His Word. Can you look back to a time when you lived to fulfill your own worldly desires like I did, but now see a clear and distinct difference in your desires as to serve God and actually live out what He commands? Are you offering your body as a living sacrifice to Him, for His kingdom and His glory? The new creature bows to the Word of God, even when it costs him his reputation and his comforts in this world, and I can assure you; it could cost him both!

The old creature loved his sin and defended it. The new creature hates his sin while he battles it. The difference is not that the old man always fails and the new man never fails; the difference is the desires of the heart. The new creature desires holiness. When you sin now, does it bring you genuine distress? Do you find yourself running *away* from temptation where you used to run *to* it? This ongoing battle is evidence of the new heart. The old creature loved self and the world. The new creature's love has been re-oriented toward God and His people. Do you sincerely love the fellowship of other believers? Do you hunger for God's presence and for the reading of His Word? Have your affections and desires been turned upside down, and now the things of God bring deep, enduring joy when in the past, you were cold to it all?

When speaking of missions, Jesus commanded us to *"Go ye therefore, and teach all nations, baptizing them in the name of the Father, and of the Son, and of the Holy Ghost"* (Matthew 28:19) The question is, who needs the message the most at this time? Is it China, India, Russia, or Indonesia? He tells us all nations, but there are SO MANY to choose from that we often get "paralysis by analysis." There is so much work to be done that we don't even know where to start, so we analyze the thing to death without ever doing anything. Struggling with this myself, I have found that the mission field that God has called me to at this time is exactly where I am at in the southeastern United States, which is often referred to as the "Bible Belt." You may think that there isn't much left to do down here since there is a church building on every corner, but there is much work to be done.

The problem here in the south is that everyone thinks they are saved. Everyone is in such close proximity to a church or church life; they feel some sense of security, whether they even go to church or not. They *"can't see the forest for the trees."* Many have not come to saving faith in Christ, continue living for the world, and couldn't care less about living their lives by the Word of God. They are not new creatures with new hearts and new desires. They are the same as they always were, unchanged and destined for Hell, and many don't even know it (I say this with all tenderness). One name could describe multitudes of people in the biblical south, and that name is Judas Iscariot. They are in such close proximity to the truth; they think that they are safe. You may ask, "How could anyone live so close to so many churches and never come to saving faith in Christ?" I would respond to that with this question, "How could Judas Iscariot spend years in close proximity to the Savior Himself and remain unchanged?"

It is a paradox. What I believe to be one of the largest mission fields on this continent is the same mission field filled with church buildings. I don't want to sound crude or cruel, and I am not attacking the church in saying this, but it is simply a fact that a lot of people that fill our local churches week after week are not new creatures. They have the outward shell of religion but not the inward reality of a new heart and new desires. There are indeed many that are genuine in their faith, that search the Scriptures to know God deeper and more intimately, and set out to live for Him. There are many beautiful souls that strive for holiness and live penitent lives for the glory of the Lamb! However, we can't turn a blind eye and pretend that we do not have goats among the sheep, and tares among the wheat.

Returning once more to our passage, it says that the old things are passed away. Is that a reality in your life? Are there things in your life that you can look back on that make you cringe today? The way you talked, or dressed, or acted towards other people? The disposition you held towards certain others? Can you truly say to yourself today that the *old you* is dead? It is not about cleaning yourself up only on Sundays to go hang out with the church crowd. Can you honestly look in the mirror and say, "By the grace of God, I am a new creature. It is evident by my new heart and new desires that the old me is passed away?"

Switching gears (but staying on the same subject): Have you ever noticed that the mirror is the most difficult place for us to find faults? It is a difficult task to search your own heart. I pray that you could find the strength to look deep into your own life, down to that place that no one else can see and examine it. Examine yourself deeply and thoroughly by the Word of God. I'm not asking you to remember the time you walked an aisle during a church service or event. I'm not asking you to remember a time or a date when someone told you that you were saved. I am asking for you to examine your heart, your motives, and your desires. Do they align with the world, or the Word? Have all things become new in your life?

I would love to say that when God saves a man, He puts a beacon or a halo on his head so that we would know without question. But we all know that isn't how He chose to work. If He did that, we would never study or try to sharpen our senses, or sharpen one another for that matter. As this book unfolds in the following chapters, it should become evident whether or not you are in the faith. We will look at foundational doctrines that have been studied and believed throughout church history. These doctrines cross denominational lines and leave few stones unturned in the quest to answer the burning question in so many hearts: "Am I saved?"

4

Different Trees, Different Fruit

In this chapter, we will take a close look into one small part of the best sermon to have ever been preached, the Sermon on the Mount. We will follow the divine logic that Jesus used to teach the people that were gathered on that day, and that He still uses to teach His people today. Sometimes, the simplest analogy can have the most profound effects on our ability to understand a concept. In this sermon, Jesus used an analogy that even a child would have had no problem understanding and grasping. It is simple, yet profound. How could *so much* truth really come from something as simple as this?

Jesus said, *"Ye shall know them by their fruits. Do men gather grapes of thorns, or figs of thistles? Even so every good tree bringeth forth good fruit; but a corrupt tree bringeth forth evil fruit. A good tree cannot bring forth evil fruit, neither can a corrupt tree bring forth good fruit. Every tree that bringeth not forth good fruit is hewn down, and cast into the fire. Wherefore by their fruits ye shall know them."* (Matthew 7:16-20)

The wisdom in these few statements is simply overwhelming! It is critical to note *why* Jesus gave this test. He was immediately following the warning to *"Beware of false prophets, which come to you in sheep's clothing, but inwardly they are ravening wolves"* (Matthew 7:15). This is the key. Since the false prophet wears a sheep's coat (meaning they have outward religion, Bible knowledge, and perhaps even works), we cannot know them by their talk or their outward appearance. The only reliable test is observing the ongoing fruit produced in their life. If this external test is necessary for identifying a false prophet, how much more so should we apply the same test to our own hearts! An underlying thought that I would ask that you keep in mind throughout the rest of this chapter is this: *By their fruits ye shall know them.*

It is a common saying, at least in the South, that you "can't judge a book by its cover." That may be true of books, but that is not necessarily true concerning people. Jesus says here that you CAN judge a book by its cover. You can look at the fruit on the limb and determine what type of tree you are looking at! The problem with us is that we need to be looking inward, and that is hard to do! As I've said, it is much easier to look outward than it is to look inward.

With a career as an industrial maintenance technician for so many years, I often approach many of the problems in my field the same way every time one arises. I identify the immediate issue at hand first, then move on to try to find the root cause of the issue. If I see that a wire is burnt in half, I can reasonably assume that I have found out why the machine stopped working. But, is repairing the burnt wire going to fix the issue? Most likely, it will not (at least for very long). There is more work to be done. I have to then identify what caused the wire to get hot and burn in the first place. I refer to the immediate concern as the "fruit," and the event that caused the immediate concern as the "root." In my professional career field, the root produces the fruit, and it is no different in the life of a man. The type of fruit that a man produces is clear evidence of the root from which he is drawing nutrients.

Do we gather grapes of thorns, or figs of thistles? Could you honestly expect to go up to an apple tree and gather blueberries? Absolutely not! The identifying factor of a tree is the fruit it bears. I know that I have four pear trees in my back yard because they make pears every year. I know that I have blueberry bushes in my back yard because in due season, they make blueberries. I know that when I go to my muscadine vine to gather the grapes, I will not get poked by thorns, because muscadine vines do not produce thorns. A tree is known by its fruit, simple as that.

To take this a step further, we need to ask ourselves a simple question. Why do pear trees make pears? The answer is just as simple as the question; because they *are* pear trees. Pear trees simply make pears because they are pear trees. If they were apple trees, they would produce apples. It's the same with any other tree. They are just doing what they do. You don't have to coerce a fruit tree or persuade it to bear its fruit. You don't have to beg a fruit tree to do what it does. If it has enough water and nutrients to stay alive, it will produce its fruit. The only way the fruit changes is if the *nature* of the tree changes. And no, you cannot rub and caress a corrupt tree into producing good fruit. To get different *fruit*, you have to draw life and sustenance from a different *root*.

Do you still have your mirror handy? Take some time to look back on your life and examine the fruit it has naturally produced. Remember, we don't beg a fruit tree to produce fruit. We simply let it produce what it produces, and determine what it is by the fruit it produces. Jesus didn't leave any room to assume that some of the trees didn't produce any fruit, so we can assuredly say that no fruit is equivalent to bad fruit. I say that because He said this;

"Every tree that bringeth not forth good fruit is hewn down, and cast into the fire." (Matthew 7:19)

No spiritual fruit is equivalent to all worldly fruit. With that being said, one can't say "I have no fruit." Remember earlier, we concluded that there are only two types of people. Here is no different. You either bear good fruit or bad fruit. If your life is marked by barrenness, you are still bearing fruit. It's just the fruit of the world and of the flesh. The Lord Jesus Himself said, *"I am the vine, ye are the branches: He that abideth in me, and I in him, the same bringeth forth much fruit: for without me ye can do nothing. If a man abide not in me, he is cast forth as a branch, and is withered; and men gather them, and cast them into the fire, and they are burned."* (John 15:5-6). By carefully examining the fruit of your life and holding it up to the light of Scripture, it will help you to discern whether you are on the narrow road, or the broad road. There are only two roads my friend, and you're on one of them!

Let's go a little further down this path while staying with the same analogy Jesus used. Would you say it is safe to assume that a tree that is fertilized, well taken care of, and pruned regularly will produce more, and even better fruit? Can we say that a fruit tree that is growing wild by itself in a thicket covered by the shade of unlike species will not produce as good as the tree that is in the orchard being well kept and pruned by the vinedresser, even if it is growing from a good root? I hope you can see that I am alluding to discipleship and to being actively surrounded by other "fruit trees" and remaining in close proximity to the Vinedresser, the Lord Jesus Christ. It is written: *"Iron sharpens iron."* Being perpetually surrounded and accompanied by Christian peers is vital for accountability and spiritual growth!

Can you reflect back on your life and see good fruit hanging from your limbs? Do you find yourself stagnant and having to constantly force yourself to produce the fruit that the Bible calls "good" or does it become easier to bear good fruit as time goes on? Can you say that you are actively pruning the limbs out of your life that you have found to be rotten? If I were to ask the person that knows you better than anyone else to write down a list of the fruit that they saw in your life on a daily basis, what would they write? Remember, *Ye shall know them by their fruit*. I wonder, by what fruit do people know you? Joy, peace, patience, soberminded, righteous, penitent, loving, and Godly? Or would it be more like dark humor, alcohol, bad language, life of the party, night life, outbursts of anger, etc.? Look in the mirror and examine yourself! The fruit of the tree always identifies the root of the tree. There are no exceptions to this. We can try to justify our "bad fruit" moments, but if you are known for being a man or woman who perpetually produces "bad fruit", that is evidence of an unchanged heart and cause for spiritual concern!

There are multitudes that go on and on in life producing what the Bible calls "bad fruit." Unless the spirit of God moves on behalf of these poor souls, they will continue in their ways. One main task of this book is to help identify and distinguish between the good fruit bearers and the bad fruit bearers. I will break it to you now; you can't live your life as a bad tree producing bad fruit and expect to be counted among the good trees during the great harvest! *"...and if the tree fall toward the south, or toward the north, in the place where the tree falleth, there it shall be."* (Ecclesiastes 11:3b)

You cannot live wrong and die right. Again, I urge you to examine yourself whether ye be in the faith! Since the Bible is

22

authoritative and inerrant, we need to be constantly saturated with the Word and conforming ourselves to that Word to be obedient children of the faith. Wouldn't it be nice to know what these good fruits look like so we can imitate them? Wouldn't it be nice to know also what the bad fruit looks like, so we can use our pruning shears and begin cutting off the rot, lest it spread to the whole tree? In the next chapter, we will look at, in detail, what the Bible defines as "good fruit" that proves the new nature, and "bad fruit" that proves otherwise. If you're honest with yourself, you will either be convicted by it or encouraged by it. It all depends on the fruit that you produce in your life. Let's continue, prayerfully.

5

Fruit of the Spirit and Sins of the Flesh

"Now the works of the flesh are manifest, which are these; Adultery, fornication, uncleanness, lasciviousness, idolatry, witchcraft, hatred, variance, emulations, wrath, strife, seditions, heresies, envyings, murders, drunkenness, revellings, and such like: of the which I tell you before, as I have also told you in time past, that they which do such things shall not inherit the kingdom of God. But the fruit of the Spirit is love, joy, peace, longsuffering, gentleness, goodness, faith, meekness, temperance: against such there is no law. And they that are Christ's have crucified the flesh with the affections and lusts. If we live in the Spirit, let us also walk in the Spirit. Let us not be desirous of vain glory, provoking one another, envying one another." (Galatians 5:19-26)

I am thankful that the Apostle Paul is the Apostle of very long lists and clear instruction! You don't have to wonder about or decode his writings! Just by reading this passage, you could almost go ahead and reach for your mirror now! If we start at the top, the first thing we see is that the works of the flesh are manifest. That's a fancy way to say that they are *not hidden*. They are out in the wide open for everyone to see, and that is very important to note. You may think that you have your sinful characteristics hidden, but they are not as far back in the closet as you would probably prefer them to be, especially from the One who sees all things. How we act and conduct ourselves really does matter and this passage gives us very clear details on what the characteristics of a lost person looks like, and also what the characteristics of a saved person looks like.

These two lists that Paul gives us are comprised of characteristics that oppose one another. The first list is the "bad fruit," and a person marked by those characteristics *shall not inherit the kingdom of God.* While the first list is not necessarily an exhaustive list of all that is sinful, it does shed light on what a sinful man looks like in a general sense. I think it would be well worth the time and ink for us to take a few of those words in the first list and unpack some of what's there. While we're at it, search your heart and life for them to be present, or anything like them! Is your life marked out by any or all of those characteristics? Are you a drunkard? Is your life marked out by hatred, strife, or envy? These are determining factors and shouldn't be read lightly or skipped over quickly.

Let's talk about a big one, idolatry! When we hear the word idolatry, we usually picture a golden calf if we're familiar with the Israelites exodus in the Old Testament. But in the New Testament, idolatry is defined as setting our affection, hope, trust, and time toward anything other than the true and living God. For many of us in the church, our idols are far more subtle and hard to detect, especially when we're trying to find them ourselves without any help!

The love of money, and the pursuit thereof, is well known to be a snare that many get caught in. While it's not sinful to have money; money does offer the opportunity to gather a lot of "stuff". And therein lies the potential problem; STUFF! The time spent chasing the money on top of the time that the "stuff" takes away is often underestimated (if it's even considered at all). In the Patriarchal period, wealth was seemingly measured by the amount of land and animals one had. In the South, the sign of wealth seems to be how much STUFF one can hoard and keep. Again, having money is not sinful, but it can lead to sinful behavior. For example: Time spent chasing money will lead you to having more money. The more money you have, the more *stuff* you can buy. Like, a boat. That boat is fun, and before you know it, you're on the lake every Sunday instead of at church. You're on the internet looking for fishing lures and watching fishing videos instead of being in the Word. And, somehow, you can "justify" it by saying things like, "Well, I work a lot of hours and I work hard! I don't have much time off, so I want to enjoy my days off!" This is a generic example, but we can be guilty of this in just about any area of life. With any hobby, whether it be hunting, fishing, sports, martial arts, etc... One thing can lead to another and you quickly run out of time. It all seems subtle and innocent, until it's not. Bible reading becomes a thing of the past, attending your local church becomes a thing of the past, and some even go so far as to avoid the church folks that they once were in communion with! Make no mistake, whatever takes up your time and attention is what you love the most!

To boil it down into simple terms, an idol is anything that takes the place of the time that you should have set apart for God, for His Word, for His people, and for His work. Fishing, hunting, sports, and the like are not sinful in and of themselves if they are put in their proper place. The problem comes when they take first place, and it takes wisdom and diligence to make sure that doesn't happen!

Another *sin of the flesh* to pay attention to is actually not "*a*" sin, but a group of them. Hatred, variance, emulations, wrath, strife, and envying. Look closely at these words. These are not directly about the body, but more so about community and relational destruction. They are the sins of the tongue and sins of the heart that can fracture families, friendships, and the local church while ruining reputations along the way. James wrote, *"Even so the tongue is a little member, and boasteth great things. Behold, how great a matter a little fire kindleth!"* (James 3:5) To be one of the smallest parts of the human body, it has the power to wreck the world!

Strife and variance will cause discord in your family (including your church family), and breeds a "divide and conquer" mentality between you and others. Envying and emulation will cause you to compare yourself to others and be resentful when someone else succeeds at something. You may try to self-promote while tearing others down. Hatred, wrath, and strife have origins in the heart, but the tongue bears its fruit. Is your life consistently characterized by these things? Do you have no plans to tear down your idols? No sorrow for your envy? No shame for your drunkenness? No desire to repent of your hatred and outbursts of anger? If so, Paul says plainly that you *"shall not inherit the kingdom of God."*

In the second list, Paul names the good fruit, what he calls the *fruit of the Spirit*. Those character traits and acts define and become the way of life for a Christian over time. As you examine yourself, can you say with confidence and assurance that your life is marked out by these qualities? Is longsuffering (patience) a characteristic of who you are? When you encounter strife, do you handle it in a calm and gentle manner seeking to make peace and reconciliation? Or, are you known for *getting back at them*, and meeting *"fire with fire"* in fits of anger? I've heard people say with my own ears that they *"just can't"* keep from blowing up with fits of anger way too often over tiny little issues and letting their emotions get the best of them. There seems to be no love for others in their hearts, and no hope or effort for them to control their negative emotions. They can go from happy to fiercely angry at the drop of a pen with little to no temperance.

The two lists Paul gives us are polar opposites. If you look into the mirror and examine your life, which set of characteristics do you see? Since we can be partial to ourselves, it may be beneficial to ask your peers that know you best to help you. Before you do, prepare yourself. If you ask an honest question, be ready for an honest answer.

Paul goes on to say that for those who live in the Spirit, we must also *walk in the Spirit* (Galatians 5:25). It is important to note that the Greek term (*stoicheo*) that was translated into the English word "walk" in this passage means to walk as in "to march in military rank," or to "keep step." The common Greek word for "walk" (as in "to move along on foot") is *(peripateo)*, but this is not the word Paul used in this passage. Paul used the word *stoicheo*.

This is not a nonchalant way of walking, or "meandering." This is not a dragging of the feet, as to merely get from one place to another. This is a type of walking that has a clear purpose behind it. When Paul says to walk in the Spirit, he means to intentionally walk with a direct and devout purpose of *marching forward* in the Spirit. Please do not take this as a passive comment from Paul. This is nothing less than a direct command that if you live in the Spirit, to also march forward in the Spirit with purpose and intent. This is a prime example of how studying Greek words can help bring a deeper meaning and understanding to the text. I'm not saying that you need to learn the entire Greek language, but having a Bible app or a good concordance to quickly reference certain words in the original language can really make an impact on your Bible study and understanding.

I want to make something clear before we get too much further. No one will ever achieve sinless perfection on this side of eternity. I am not saying that a true Christian will never have another outburst of anger. I am not saying that a Christian will never have another sinful thought. I am not saying that a Christian will be meek and loving every second of every day for the rest of their lives, or that a Christian will be perfectly patient every time they are tested. I understand that some of this may come across to you as "legalistic," but please bear with me to the end before making that assumption. The crucial difference between a saved person and a lost person is not the presence of sin, but rather the pattern and the response to sin! Our *marching* with the Spirit will not be without slips, trips, falls, and shortcomings. It is a war with the flesh, but we are all called to march forward into the battle toward holiness!

6

Chastened, as a Son?

You may be apprehensive to continue on by the title of this chapter, but we must go on. This is a subject that is much like the doctrines of repentance and election in the modern mega-church age, forgotten and/or ignored altogether. No one really seems excited to talk about chastisement or being disciplined, and I have to admit that I am right there with you. It is not as joyous of a topic as love, forgiveness, grace, or mercy. However, we find it clearly in Scripture, so we cannot ignore it just because we do not like it. It's in there, so we must discuss it. By discussing it, it can prove to be a determining factor for us, whether we are in the faith or not. With that being said, let us proceed thoughtfully and carefully.

"For whom the Lord loveth he chasteneth, and scourgeth every son whom he receiveth. If ye endure chastening, God dealeth with you as with sons; for what son is he whom the father chasteneth not? But if ye be without chastisement, whereof all are partakers, then are ye bastards, and not sons. Furthermore we have had fathers of our flesh which corrected us, and we gave them reverence: shall we not much rather be in subjection unto the Father of spirits, and live? For they verily for a few days chastened us after their own pleasure; but he for our profit, that we might be partakers of his holiness. Now no chastening for the present seemeth to be joyous, but grievous: nevertheless afterward it yieldeth the peaceable fruit of righteousness unto

them which are exercised thereby. Wherefore lift up the hands which hang down, and the feeble knees; And make straight paths for your feet, lest that which is lame be turned out of the way; but let it rather be healed. Follow peace with all men, and holiness, without which no man shall see the Lord:" (Hebrews 12:6-14)

The first thing I would like to do is again return to the original language to see what some of these uncommon English words mean. The word "chasteneth" comes from the Greek word (*paideuo*) that literally means to train up a child, as *to educate* or *by discipline*. The English word "scourgeth" comes from the Greek word (*mastigoo*) which means to literally or figuratively *flog*. I can remember from a young age that my aunt would always threaten to "flog" me if I didn't stop whatever I was doing that preceded her threat. Verily, verily, I say unto thee; I did not know that *flog* was a real word at that time. I thought it was something that she made up to scare me. Turns out, it really is a word. Because of my own disobedience, I was often treated as a canoe. You know the old saying, "for best results, paddle from the rear." I didn't care for it too much back then, but it helped to *steer* me in the right direction.

In our passage, we can see that our Heavenly Father also chastens and scourges every son that He receives. *EVERY son...* In fact, in the following verse, the writer of Hebrews says that if you endure chastening, then God is dealing with you as a son. What can we say about a son whose father doesn't discipline him? As I am both a parent and a child, I can say with certainty that my parents cared enough for me to discipline me, and I also care enough about my child to discipline her. For a parent to let their children run free with no discipline is a sure way to end up with a heathen, and a menace to society! We see in other passages that if you do not discipline your children, it means that you *hate* them. Strong, but true words! *"He that spareth his rod hateth his son: but he that loveth him chasteneth him betimes."* (Proverbs 13:24)

This resonates with our passage in Hebrews, because in the very next words, the writer says that if you are not being chastened by the Father, you are bastards, and not sons. I would like to pretend that all parents discipline their children to an extent, but I know that is not true. I lay the blame of the degradation of this society squarely at the feet of the parents who refused to discipline their children. As long as passive parents abound, Satan has no need to come up with extraordinary means to carry out his schemes. Parents who refuse to discipline and exercise authority over their children are Satan's chief tools to shape the next generation. Let it be known that if you want to work against God, simply let your children run free! Your neutrality in parenting will come back to bite eventually, whether that be you in this generation, or someone else in the next...

On the human side of this predicament, neither side enjoys scourging. Neither the one giving, nor the one receiving. But, as our passage says, afterwards it yields good fruit! Chastisement is a means by which our Heavenly Father brings out the good fruit in us. It is an act of pruning and shaping of the vine (us) by the Vinedresser (Him). I have long rows of muscadine grape vines on my property and I often go out to trim off the dead vines to clean them up to make them presentable and actually give them the ability to bear good fruit. If there are too many vines for the root system, there will be less fruit and they are more susceptible to fungus and disease. You can apply this analogy to the Christian life. When we get too many things going on and end up short on time, do not be surprised if God comes by to trim some *overgrowth* out of your life so that you can bear good fruit. This could be an example of being chastened.

Our earthly parents chastened us after their own limited pleasure, but God chastens us for our ultimate profit as the passage states, *"that we might be partakers of his holiness."* In a parental sense, we discipline our children with the goal of conforming them into sane, respectful, and productive members of our society. We have a feeling of accomplishment in our children when they go out into the world and make positive impacts and do good things. In our minds, we have succeeded in something that we wanted for them. In a spiritual sense, our Heavenly Father disciplines us to accomplish one of His missions in our personal lives, which is to conform us to the image of His Son (Romans 8:29). If we do it for our children, how much more so would God be willing to "raise His children in discipline" to go out into the world and accomplish His mission?

Consider Jacob and Esau in this regard. *"As it is written, Jacob have I loved, but Esau have I hated."* (Romans 9:13) How did God show hatred towards Esau and love toward Jacob? God let Esau run wild and do as he pleased by following the desires of his flesh without consequences. On the other hand, He showed His love towards Jacob by *flogging* him on a regular basis (literally and figuratively). Jacob's life was marked by hardship, betrayal, wrestling with God, and constant refinement. It was all orchestrated to burn off the chaff of his fraud and make him the Godly man who would eventually become Israel. One sure mark of a true Christian is this; regularly being chastened as a son.

What does chastisement look like for a believer today? It is not always a major illness or tragedy, and you may not end up with a limp like Jacob had, though it could be exactly that. More often, it's subtle things that we really need to be aware of and attentively looking for. Chastisement can be things like providential frustration and persistent conviction. If you find that you see an open door that would be so easy to walk through, but God in his providence keeps closing that door for you, that could be a sign that you shouldn't be there at this time in your life. If you are burdened by a loss of a job or relationship, that could be God teaching you to stop relying on yourself and to rely on Him. Maybe your conscience is burdened by the Scriptures over a secret or ongoing sin that you are hanging on to, so much that you can't seem to get a good night's sleep over it. This pricking of the conscience and internal distress is probably a form of discipline, especially if you haven't ever felt the way you do now over the same issue. As we grow in the grace and knowledge of God, He will shape our lives along the way, and many times, it can be painful. But it yields good fruit!

Another form of spiritual discipline is suffering. *"But the God of all grace, who hath called us unto his eternal glory by Christ Jesus, after that ye have suffered a while, make you perfect, stablish, strengthen, settle you."* (1 Peter 5:10) This is an extremely sensitive subject. If you have been on this earth for more than about fifteen minutes, you've experienced suffering, at least to some extent. God sees it fit to put some people through a lot more than others. I have had my share of suffering, both physically and emotionally. I've gone through the deaths of family members and close friends, physical health problems, financial struggles, etc. But if I take a close look at my life and compared it to some others, I have had a walk in the park.

34

The theologian John Owen (1616-1683) endured through the death of almost all eleven of his children in infancy. He then lost his first wife, Mary, after 32 years of marriage, all while struggling with chronic health issues, including asthma and gallstones. He also was persecuted politically, lost his public influence, and struggled with heavy spiritual discouragement. Even through all of his suffering while he was on this earth, he left his mark of resilience and managed to write many impactful books that are still available today, including titles like; *"The Mortification of Sin"*, *"The Death of Death"*, and many others.

Another example of suffering is the life of the successful lawyer and businessman of Chicago, Horatio Spafford (1828-1888). He lost most of his fortune in the great Chicago fire of 1871. Then, he lost all four daughters in a shipwreck while they and his wife were on their way across the Atlantic in 1873. His wife, Anna, was the sole survivor of their family in the shipwreck. When she arrived at her destination, she sent a message to her husband back in Chicago that read only these words; "saved alone." This is an example of extreme suffering, but also a story of unwavering faith. As Mr. Spafford was aboard a ship on his way to be reunited with his mourning wife, they crossed the area of the shipwreck and while looking out across the open sea where his daughters died just days before, he penned the line to what would become one of the most well-known and powerful hymns to have ever been written;

When peace like a river attendeth my way,
when sorrows like sea billows roll;
whatever my lot, thou hast taught me to say,
"It is well, it is well with my soul."

All of this suffering is for a purpose. The passage in 1 Peter states that suffering is required, at least to an extent, to *"make you perfect, stablish, strengthen, settle you."* Suffering isn't a light subject and it isn't something that we like to welcome with open arms, but it is a means that God uses to work in the lives of His people.

Oh mirror, mirror! Where are you? As we reflect upon our own lives, can you see the Father at work in your life in the form of discipline? When hardship comes, is your first response to rebel and curse God, or to fall on your face and ask, "Lord, what are you teaching me?" Does your conscience scream at you when you know you are doing wrong according to Scripture? Have you noticed, by the providence of God, that you are unable to run wild as a heathen? Are you being conformed to the image of His Son, or do you look like the world around you? Do the things of this world soothe your soul, or does it turn to gravel in your gut? These are questions that we should all reflect on, deeply and thoroughly.

This is the great difference: The true child, though momentarily hurting, eventually submits to the Father's hand and is humbled and strengthened by the experience. The reprobate, when disciplined, simply hardens his heart and runs further away. If you are suffering through trials and discipline, I would admonish you to run to and submit to God. He is more than willing and more than able to comfort and guide His children.

7

Repentance

Father, forgive us, for we have sinned… This is yet another topic that rarely makes it to the table for discussion in modern church life. We speak much on the love of God, and we should continue to do so regularly. The Word doesn't only say that God loves, but goes so far as to say that God *"is love."* (1 John 4:8, 1 John 4:16) Love is not only what He does, but it is the very essence of who He is. No wonder it is such a frequently studied topic! It deserves to be, since it can offer comfort and hope to the believer! Love is also a defining characteristic of Christians, but we will discuss that topic in more detail later. For this chapter, we have to look at the doctrine of repentance and why it is so crucial in the Christian life. Throughout church history, faith and repentance have been considered to be two of the greatest graces gifted by God to sinners. They are two graces in which the Christian grows and matures over the course of their lives. Thomas Watson (1620-1686) said that "faith and repentance are the two wings by which a Christian flies to Heaven." (paraphrased)

First of all, I want to define the term itself. The English word repent comes from a compound Greek word (Transliteration: *metanoeo*) that literally means to *think differently*, or simply to reconsider. That is the literal definition of the word, but the action is much more profound. When a person is regenerated and is made alive to spiritual matters, their mind is renewed, and they begin to see God, sin, and self through a much different lens. Sin is no longer a pleasure, but a poison.

My personal interpretation of the act of repenting is as follows: To turn from as much as you know of sin, to give as much as you know of yourself, to as much as you know of God. This turning is the action that follows the changed thinking. Repentance is not merely feeling sad about your actions; it is a reorientation of the will. It is common for church folks to only use the word repent in the past tense form "repented." I can't say that I haven't used it that way myself. While that is important and hopefully true, repentance is not a singular event that is done once and departed from. It's not like a trophy you get at the end of a race or an event. Repentance is not like a baptism, in that it only happens once. Repentance is not a sacrament. Repentance is not a prayer. Repentance is a way of life, and a defining characteristic of a true Christian.

Some people have a "knee-jerk" reaction when things get bad. They find themselves in the storms of life and in desperation cry out for salvation. They make pleas with God and superficial deals with themselves to turn from whatever ailed them or got them into their predicament. This is an example of worldly sorrow, which we will discuss in a short while, but this is not true repentance. This is an act of desperation to escape the consequences of a bad situation. This type of false repentance was likely birthed during the storms of life, but will ultimately fade away when the storm passes.

When we say that a person is penitent, we are saying that person lives in a perpetual state of repentance. This is not for the faint of heart. Battling with the flesh and keeping the "old man" subdued is hard work. The Puritans would often compare repentance to digging for precious metals. While it is hard work and may cause you to sweat, is not the reward in the end worthy of the labor? The true believer is always digging deeper, always recognizing more and more error in their ways, and always relying more and more on Christ and resting in His finished work.

To let Scripture make the case for itself, let me mention a few passages to show the importance and tangible reality of the doctrine of repentance. If we look at Jesus' public ministry, we see that repentance is a thread unbroken from the beginning to the end. What are the first recorded words that we have of John the Baptist? *"Repent ye, for the kingdom of heaven is at hand."* (Matthew 3:2) What about the first words of Jesus in His public ministry? *"The time is fulfilled, the kingdom of God is at hand, repent ye and believe the Gospel."* (Mark 1:15) And in His farewell address just before He ascended to heaven, He said that *"repentance and remission of sins should be preached in His name among all nations, beginning at Jerusalem."* (Luke 24:47)

Since Jesus Christ Himself preached repentance coming and going, it should be very important for us to take note. The disciples also preached this as He sent them out two by two. *"And they went out, and preached that men should repent."* (Mark 6:12) Peter did not soon forget the mission, as we also see that he was consistent in preaching repentance in the second chapter of Acts. Guilty parties seemed to be present before Peter at the time of this sermon. *"Him, being delivered by the determinate counsel and foreknowledge of God, ye have taken, and by wicked hands have crucified and slain."* (Acts 2:23) Are you wondering how the wicked men responded to Peter's message? *"Now when they heard this, they were pricked in their heart, and said unto Peter and to the rest of the apostles, Men and brethren, what shall we do?"* (Acts 2:37)

Notice the passage says that they were pricked in their heart. That is the evidence of a change on the inside of a man. That is the evidence of the Holy Spirit of God giving sinful men the ability to see the truth. They were under conviction, but they still had a big problem. They suddenly came to the knowledge that they were wrong, but they didn't know what to do about it, so they asked what they needed to do. They wanted to *"do something"* to make it right. (Does this sound familiar?) So, what did Peter instruct the wicked men to do? *"Then Peter said unto them, Repent, and be baptized every one of you in the name of Jesus Christ for the remission of sins, and ye shall receive the gift of the Holy Ghost."* (Acts 2:38)

Now that we know what the word means, and we know that it was preached and taught by Jesus, the disciples, and the apostles, we are left with one crucial question for assurance, and that is: "What sorrow accompanies true repentance?" Wouldn't you know it! Scripture has all the answers we need. *"All Scripture is given by inspiration of God, and is profitable for doctrine, for reproof, for correction, for instruction in righteousness: that the man of God may be perfect, thoroughly furnished unto all good works."* (2 Timothy 3:16-17) To answer the question, we need to look to the Apostle Paul's second epistle to the Corinthians: *"For godly sorrow worketh repentance to salvation not to be repented of: but the sorrow of the world worketh death."* (2 Corinthians 7:10)

This is the great distinguishing mark. There can be two kinds of sorrow when we sin. There is worldly sorrow and Godly sorrow. Worldly sorrow focuses only on the consequences of sin.

40

When we experience worldly sorrow, it produces despair and anger. That ultimately leads to a hardened heart, especially if the guilty party doesn't *"get away"* with their shenanigans. This is the sorrow of Judas Iscariot. But Godly sorrow is a sorrow much different than worldly sorrow. Godly sorrow focuses on the offense toward a holy God. Godly sorrow is grief over sin because of who God is, not because of the worldly consequences you may experience because of committing the vile act against Him and His Word. Godly sorrow leads to a desire to change, *"not to be repented of."*

The true child of God, when under conviction, responds with inward godly sorrow. We see this with the Publican in the temple. In Luke chapter eighteen, we read about the two men who went up the temple to pray. First, the Pharisee who went up to pray and declared all the wonderful things that he had done, and how content he was in that he wasn't like the others. And then we read, *"And the publican, standing afar off, would not lift up so much as his eyes unto heaven, but smote upon his breast, saying, God be merciful to me a sinner."* (Luke 18:13)

Jesus goes on to say that this publican went on justified, unlike the other. What happened to that publican? A deep conviction of sin came over him to the point that he wouldn't even lift his head, but could only *smite upon his breast* and cry out for mercy. He was cut to the very core by the truth. It is not quite time for you to pick up your mirror, but you can ask yourself, "Am I like the Pharisee, or the Publican? You can also read the Parable of the Prodigal Son in your own time (Luke 15:11-32), and as you do so, pay special attention to verse 17 where it says, *"And when he came to himself..."* Has there ever been a time that you can reflect on in your life when you finally *"came to yourself"* as this

41

rebellious son did? Have you ever been running wild and squandering your life away by enjoying the pleasures of this world, and then been found under heavy conviction of your sin and riotous living? Have you ever cried out to God, "Be merciful to me, a sinner?"

This business of repentance is not a peripheral doctrine for some to follow and others to ignore. It is purely a Gospel grace that is necessary for all God's people. If your life is void of this *metanoeo*, your life is void of the Savior. God's people repent, period. Not because it is required for salvation, but because He gives you the inclination to realize it, the will to want it, and the power to do it. *"And the times of this ignorance God winked at; but now commandeth all men every where to repent"* (Acts 17:30) Is repentance evident in your life? This is a defining mark of a true Christian. If I could conclude this chapter with a vehement exhortation, I would quote John the Baptist and say, *"Repent ye: for the kingdom of heaven is at hand."* (Matthew 3:2)

8

Am I Being Sanctified?

"And the very God of peace sanctify you wholly; and I pray God your whole spirit and soul and body be preserved blameless unto the coming of our Lord Jesus Christ." (1 Thessalonians 5:23)

"But we are bound to give thanks alway to God for you, brethren beloved of the Lord, because God hath from the beginning chosen you to salvation through sanctification of the Spirit and belief of the truth" (2 Thessalonians 2:13)

"Sanctify them through thy truth: thy word is truth" (John 17:17)

If you have stayed with this book so far, you should have a solid foundation for the answer to the important question, "How am I saved?" The answer is clear: by faith alone in the finished work of Jesus Christ alone. Being justified legally is what gives us peace with God.

But here is where many Christians get stuck, leading to the question this chapter addresses. If salvation is real, why do I still struggle so much with sin? If I was made a "new creature," why does the "old man" keep showing up and causing trouble and leading me astray? Confusion, doubt, and lack of assurance often happen because we mix up two very different but equally glorious works of God. These are the doctrine of Justification and the doctrine of Sanctification. We need to clearly separate them, because if they get blurred, you will always look at your own imperfect performance for your assurance, and you will never find true peace. When we talk about the great salvation God gives us, we often use these two words. Understanding the difference between them is the key to assurance.

The first is "Justification", an immediate act of God whereby the eternal penalty of sin is removed. This is a singular point in time when we are declared righteous in a legal sense. Think of it like a judge declaring you "not guilty," and more importantly, declaring you perfectly righteous because your sin debt has been paid and Christ's perfect righteousness has been credited to your account. It happens instantly and completely the moment you put your faith in Jesus Christ. It is a spiritual work that changes your legal standing before God. Your standing never gets better, and it never gets worse. It is finished and secure the moment you believe. *"Therefore being justified by faith, we have peace with God through our Lord Jesus Christ."* (Romans 5:1)

The second is "Sanctification", an ongoing act of God whereby the power of indwelling sin is being removed throughout the life of the believer. Sanctification is the daily, continuous process of being made holy and becoming more and more like Christ. It is an internal work that changes your character and conduct. If justification is God *declaring* you righteous, sanctification is God *making* you righteous throughout your daily life.

The Bible uses the word sanctification directly. The Greek word for sanctification (*hagiasmos*) simply means to be *set apart*, or *distinct*. You were initially set apart from the world unto God (positional sanctification), and now, you are being set apart from sin and unto righteousness in your daily life (progressive sanctification). This process is co-operative. While the Holy

Spirit is the one who gives you the ability and the desire to follow God, you are responsible for using the means of grace to *"...work out your own salvation with fear and trembling. For it is God which worketh in you both to will and to do of his good pleasure."* (Philippians 2:12–13)

Notice the balance. You work *out* (your duty) what God works *in* (His grace). You are justified by faith alone, but you are sanctified by faith and effort. Your sanctification is the evidence of your justification, NEVER the cause of it. And make no mistake, friends, to *"mortify the deeds of the body"* is a daily war, but a work that's well worth the sweat. Sanctification is not a suggestion, but a necessity, as the writer of Hebrews warns: *"Follow peace with all men, and holiness, without which no man shall see the Lord."* (Hebrews 12:14).

The word *holiness* here is also (*hagiasmos*), which is translated to English as "sanctification" just as often as it is "holiness" in the *Textus Receptus*. A life completely void of this ongoing, observable process is evidence of an unsaved heart. Since sanctification is progressive (slow and steady), how do you know if you are moving at all? You shouldn't look for perfection, but you must look for direction. Hold up your life to the looking-glass of God's Word and examine your heart against these evidences.

The first undeniable evidence of sanctification is a persistent and intentional war against sin. The true Christian cannot comfortably coexist with their former lusts. *"For if ye live after the flesh, ye shall die: but if ye through the Spirit do mortify the deeds of the body, ye shall live."* (Romans 8:13) To *mortify* is translated from the Greek (*thanatoo*), which literally means to "put to death" or "make dead." This is an active command. It is not an invitation to passively wait for sin to leave, but a demand to actively slay sinful habits. If you were truly set free from the penalty of sin, you should be fighting daily to be set free from the power and presence of indwelling sin.

Have you thrown your mirror away? Hopefully not! Pick it up and look deeply into the life that only you can see. Do you treat your sins as beloved pets or as mortal enemies? Is there a relentless, uncomfortable pressure in your life to abandon the things that you know God hates? It's sad to say, but sin is present in every one of our lives whether we like to admit it or not, but the difference is this: The lost man is defined by the domination and love of sin, but the saved man is defined by the hatred and warfare against it.

The second evidence of sanctification is not only about actively putting off the works of the flesh. It is also about actively putting on the righteous character of Christ. This character is summarized by the fruit that the Holy Spirit naturally produces in a believer. *"But the fruit of the Spirit is love, joy, peace, longsuffering, gentleness, goodness, faith, meekness, temperance: against such there is no law."* (Galatians 5:22–23) Notice that the word *fruit* is singular. These nine qualities are one inseparable evidence of the Spirit's presence. The question is not whether you are perfectly manifesting them all, but whether they are the trajectory of your life. Is your default setting, over time, shifting from impatience to longsuffering? From anxiety to peace? If a person who knows you well were asked to describe your dominant traits, would love, joy, and peace be mentioned, or would they say anger, bitterness, and selfishness?

The third evidence of sanctification is being sustained by a continuous growth in understanding God's Word and the increasing reliance on His grace. *"But grow in grace, and in the knowledge of our Lord and Savior Jesus Christ…"* (2 Peter 3:18) How do we gain knowledge of God and get to know Him better? By studying His Word. End of story. If your Bible is untouched and living on a shelf, the dust on its cover bears witness against you!

If your relationship with Christ is authentic, it will not be static. The true vine produces an ever-increasing yield. This growth is evidenced by a deepening hunger for the Word and a greater reliance on the Person of Christ rather than your own efforts. You will recognize that grace is both the undeserved favor of God that saves you, and the daily power of God that sustains you and helps you obey. Look into the mirror of your life. Is your Bible reading stagnant? Do you treasure God's word above your necessary food (Job 23:12)? Does the idea of knowing Christ better excite you, or is your spiritual life a matter of repetitive obligation? Growth may be slow, but it must be present. A tree that does not grow is a dead tree.

The fourth evidence of sanctification is becoming more humble and more contrite. The more a person grows in sanctification, the more they realize how short they fall of God's standard (which is perfection). A sanctified person does not look down their nose at others, but rather looks at the purity of Christ and is humbled and broken by their own continued sinfulness. A religious pretender boasts about his works, but a genuine saint marvels and often weeps with gratitude at God's mercy and grace. True sanctification strips away pride and replaces it with humility and a constant, desperate reliance on Christ. *"…but to this man will I look, even to him that is poor and of a contrite spirit, and trembleth at my word."* (Isaiah 66:2)

If you find that the deeper you dive into Scripture, the less impressed you are with yourself and the more magnificent Christ appears, then you have clear evidence of the Holy Spirit's work. The process of sanctification is a spiritual discipline, not a means of earning salvation. Recognizing a pattern of sanctification in your life can help to confirm the genuine work of God, who promises that, *"He which hath begun a good work in you will perform it until the day of Jesus Christ."* (Philippians 1:6)

If you are fighting sin, if you are seeing the fruit of the Spirit, and if you are growing in grace and humility, you have strong, Scriptural evidence that you are indeed being sanctified and that the great work of salvation is continuing in you. Take a moment now and prayerfully consider these three summarizing questions: Am I actively fighting and mourning over my sin, or have I made peace with certain transgressions? Is the observable trajectory of my character one of increasing love, joy, and peace (fruits of the Spirit)? Am I hungry for the knowledge of Christ and actively growing in my understanding of God and His grace?

9

The Marks of Peace, Love, and Joy

In the last chapter, we looked in the mirror seeking marks of sanctification, which is the ongoing, progressive work of the Holy Spirit making us more like Christ. But what exactly does that new character look like? It is not merely the absence of sin, but the positive presence of spiritual attributes and virtues. The Apostle Paul gives us an extensive list of the Spirit's fruit in Galatians 5:22: *"But the fruit of the Spirit is love, joy, peace, longsuffering, gentleness, goodness, faith, meekness, temperance..."* The first three marks are love, joy, and peace. These are fundamental indicators of the Spirit's indwelling. They are not temporary emotions you manufacture, but the natural evidence of a root system planted firmly in the Gospel. If these three marks are present in your life, even imperfectly, they speak volumes to the question, "Am I saved?" Let us hold our lives up to the Scriptures and examine ourselves, seeking out these three Gospel graces in particular.

The person who has been justified is also the person who experiences a supernaturally secure and settled peace. The first, greatest peace you receive is peace with God, which is the end of hostility (Romans 5:1). The peace we examine here is the peace of God, not worldly peace. Worldly peace is defined simply as the absence of conflict or worry. It lasts only until the next bill arrives or the next bad news breaks. The peace of God, however, is an inner security that remains steady in the midst of the storm. Paul describes this peace in Philippians 4:7, *"And the peace of God, which passeth all understanding, shall keep your hearts and minds through Christ Jesus."*

The Greek word for this divine peace is (*eirene*). It does not only mean "quietness" but a state of wholeness, harmony, and well-being. It is the comprehensive completeness that comes from knowing the sovereign God as your Father, your Savior, and your Keeper. It is a peace that your mind cannot fully comprehend because it defies our human logic. How can you be calm when the trial is raging? How could John Owen keep pressing on while dealing with all of his trials? What about Horatio Spafford? How could he hold it together through his life of storms? The answer is that their peace was anchored in the Person of Christ, not defined by their circumstances. This peace protects your two most precious inner faculties: Your heart (which is the seat of emotion and will) and your mind (which is the seat of thought and reason).

When trials or distress come, is your default setting one of panic and despair, or do you have a core, unshakeable confidence that God is still in control? Do you experience a sense of rest even when your circumstances are chaotic? We often take what we call "bad situations" and label them as an attack from Satan, or in the very least, a "test" from God. Whatever it truly is, be sure of this: God is still on the throne, God allowed and ordained it, and He works ALL THINGS together for good to those who are called according to His purpose! (Romans 8:28)

The fruit of the Spirit is also defined by love. If a believer does not manifest love, the other fruits cannot truly exist. We must distinguish here, however, between God's general love for all of creation and His special, covenantal, and electing love for His redeemed. If your assurance is based on an emotional feeling that God "must" love you, it is fragile at best. Assurance must be rooted in the unshakable, purposeful nature of God's redemptive and active choice. This is the solid rock of proper theology. God's love for the believer is not a sentimental preference, but an unchanging attribute, demonstrated in a definitive act! *"But God commendeth his love toward us, in that, while we were yet sinners, Christ died for us."* (Romans 5:8)

God's love is not primarily felt, but it is also demonstrated by the cross. The love produced as fruit in the believer is (*agape*). This is one of the Greek words that we really need to understand. *Agape* is not a passionate, romantic, or even a familial love. It is the active, intentional, self-sacrificial love that chooses the highest good of the object, regardless of the cost or the object's merit. It is the type of love Christ showed on the cross. When God the Holy Spirit dwells in you, He begins to align your will with His will, giving you the desire to love others with this *agape* love. This love will persevere through fights and squabbles, forgive those who offend you, and actively seek the good of your peers, and even your enemies.

The Greek language is much different than English, and we truly received the short end of the stick on this one! In English, we say that we "love" our spouse and that we "love" our parents. But we also say that we "love" pizza and tacos. We use the one word universally, but the Greek has up to eight words that describe different types, or "levels" of love, and *Agape* (the word Paul used for love in Romans 5:8) is the one that describes unconditional, selfless, benevolent love. THAT love is the fruit of the Spirit according to Galatians 5:22.

When a fellow Christian or a difficult neighbor offends you, is your first instinct to withdraw and retaliate, or to actively seek their spiritual good with grace and meekness? Does your love for God motivate you to obey His Word and walk circumspectly, or is your "love" merely an experience-based emotion of a warm, fleeting feeling during a worship song? These are crucial distinctions that must be sorted out, and can only be sorted out when we examine ourselves closely, and without prejudice.

Another mark of the Spirit's work is joy. Joy is often used interchangeably with happiness in the world, but the two are separated by a wide chasm of spiritual significance. Happiness is an emotion that depends on immediate happenings or circumstances. If something good happens, like you get a pay raise, the sun is shining, your health is good, then you are happy. Dopamine and serotonin are circulating around in your system. Your mood is elevated and your brain is rewarded. LIFE IS GREAT! But happiness is a temporary visitor. Hormone levels ebb and flow like the sea, rise and fall like the great rulers of this world. Happiness is nothing more than an influx of hormones, and that's all it is. Happiness is not an anchor to hold on to. Happiness is not a litmus test to judge character. Happiness, again, is a temporary visitor that often leaves much too soon. But joy…

Joy (*chara*), which shares a root with grace (*charis*), is a deep-seated, constant character trait that is rooted in the unchanging truth of God's grace in salvation. It is an unexplainable spiritual endowment. A person can be experiencing great suffering, or the temporary loss of all worldly happiness, yet still possess deep, spiritual joy. Why? Because the source and substance of Christian joy is immutable (unchangeable). It is the finished work of Christ and the assurance of God's presence and promises. Joy, therefore, is not a feeling; it is a strong characteristic of the Christian life. As Nehemiah 8:10 says: *"...for the joy of the LORD is your strength."* This joy gives you the fortitude to endure trials, to confess sin, and to persevere in and endure the process of sanctification. You are joyful because your name is written in Heaven (Luke 10:20), not because your bank account is full. This constant character trait confirms the Spirit's presence. For a true Christian, their face may be long and hang low at times, but their joy is everlasting.

Grab your mirror and self-reflect. When troubles multiply, what is the well that you draw from? Is your inner well dry until your circumstances improve, or can you find contentment and strength in Christ while your world is falling apart? These three graces; peace, love, and joy are not options. They are the necessary, inseparable fruits produced when the Holy Spirit takes residence in a new creature. If you are a Christian struggling with the question, "Am I saved?", stop looking at your momentary failures and instead look at the trail of your life and the source of your affections. If you possess a peace that defies your circumstances, an agape love that motivates obedience to God and peace towards your fellow man, and an unshakable joy that remains steadfast through trials, then you have observable evidence that you have indeed been set apart, you are being sanctified, and you are secure in Christ!

10

Perseverance

To this point in this writing, we have taken a biblical look at what a man or woman of God should look like according to Scripture, while kicking the emotional aspect out the back door. It goes without saying, but emotions are powerful. We can let our emotions lead us to say, feel, and ultimately believe something to be true when it is not. When Christ enters the heart of a man, of course emotions change, but being born again is so much more than emotion. It is a tangible change whereby EVERYTHING is made new, both immediately and over time. I hope that I have helped anyone who reads this to see and better understand that fact by looking at the Word of God instead of the ideas and opinions of man.

Now we arrive at another crucial observation, and that is endurance. It is common to hear of a person who "made a decision for Christ," only to see them walk away from the faith years later. This raises the painful question; Were they ever saved to begin with? The final mark of a saved soul that I want to discuss in this writing is perseverance. This is unshakeable evidence that a work of God was truly done in the heart of a man. Our Lord Jesus Christ made it clear that salvation is not a temporary experience, but a final state confirmed by a lifelong journey: *"But, he that shall endure unto the end, the same shall be saved."* (Matthew 24:13) The one who truly has the new life of Christ will continue in the faith. The Greek word translated as endure is (*hupomenō*). This word is incredibly rich. It means "to remain under", or to "take patiently." It is not passive resignation, but active, committed patience in the face of pressure, affliction, and all manner of temptation.

The doctrine of the "Perseverance of the Saints" does not teach that the true believer is somehow strong enough to hold onto Christ. It teaches the opposite, that God is strong enough to hold onto the believer. Let me put it to you this way if you are truly saved: If it was up to you to keep yourself saved, you would have lost your salvation before you finished reading this sentence. Since salvation is entirely God's work, He who began the good work will bring it to completion (Philippians 1:6). Our endurance, therefore, is the evidence of His work, not the cause of our salvation. Oftentimes we judge our standing in our own ability to walk according to the Scriptures, but this is putting the "cart before the horse". Us having the ability to walk according to the Spirit is His work, too. The true believer will endure while the false believer will ultimately fall away. This truth is powerfully demonstrated in one of Christ's most vital lessons.

To help us distinguish between true faith and temporary excitement, Christ told the Parable of the Sower (Matthew 13:3–23). A sower scattered seed upon four different types of ground. Three types failed to bring forth fruit because they lacked something. This parable is a perfect place to pick up the mirror for our self-examination. Look closely at your own spiritual life and compare your own walk to these four grounds: The wayside, the stony ground, the thorny ground, and the good ground.

"When any one heareth the word of the kingdom, and understandeth it not, then cometh the wicked one, and catcheth away that which was sown in his heart. This is he which received seed by the way side." (Matthew 13:19)

The wayside (*hodos*) is "the road," or a trampled-down path. The seed never penetrates the surface, but is snatched away instantly. This represents the reprobate who hears the Gospel but never truly understands its eternal weight, value, or application. There is no conviction, no change, and consequently, no endurance. The question for you is: Has the Word of God ever actually penetrated and broken your heart? Does the message of the cross immediately bounce off, leaving your heart just as cold and hard as it was before?

Next is the stony ground. *"But he that received the seed into stony places, the same is he that heareth the word, and anon with joy receiveth it; Yet hath he not root in himself, but dureth for a while: for when tribulation or persecution ariseth because of the word, by and by he is offended."* (Matthew 13:20–21)

The stony ground is the most deceptive. The seed sprouts quickly because the soil is shallow. It is warmed easily by the sun. This represents an emotional, superficial conversion. This is what happened to me as a teen, when I took it upon myself to walk the aisle. The person receives the word with joy, perhaps enjoying the fellowship, the music, or the good feelings of a church service. They have no root in Christ and they are not born again. As soon as tribulation (*thlipsis*), meaning pressure, anguish, affliction, or persecution arises, their temporary faith withers. Their "faith" *dureth for a while*, but it will not endure through the storms of life. This failure to persevere is the undeniable mark of the reprobate who was never truly saved. Has your faith been tested by pain, mocking, suffering, or loss? When life became truly difficult and hard to reason with, did you run to Christ for safety, or did you run away from Him, blaming Him for the things you didn't understand?

The thorny ground… *"He also that received seed among the thorns is he that heareth the word; and the care of this world, and the deceitfulness of riches, choke the word, and he becometh unfruitful."* (Matthew 13:22)

This ground is tragic because the seed grows alongside the weeds. This person truly hears and may even experience a level of conviction and a troubled conscience, but a troubled conscience is not sufficient for repentance, and it doesn't equate to salvation. They love the world just as much, if not more, than they love God. They try to serve two masters, which Christ promised cannot be done (Matthew 6:24). Their love for the cares of this world, whether it be their job, their social status, their bank account, or their entertainment, acts like thorns, growing faster and stronger until the spiritual life is suffocated. The ultimate result is that they become unfruitful. They did not endure, because their passion was divided and without focus.

If this sounds like you, answer this question: What is choking the life out of your relationship with Christ? Are your time, energy, and efforts consumed by the pursuits of this world, leaving only leftovers for God? Do you find yourself consistently prioritizing temporary comforts over eternal commitment? These are vital questions we must ask ourselves often. This is part of *"working out our own salvation with fear and trembling."* It takes time, effort, and diligence, but it is well worth the effort. If you misplaced a thousand dollars cash, how much time and effort would you spend looking for it? I can assume that you're like me; I would look until I found it! How much time and effort do you spend seeking after God in His Word? I can tell you that whatever you spend your free time on is what you love the most.

And now, the good ground! *"But he that received seed into the good ground is he that heareth the word, and understandeth it; which also beareth fruit, and bringeth forth, some an hundredfold, some sixty, some thirty."* (Matthew 13:23)

The good ground is the only place the seed finds true life. This represents the person who hears, understands, and receives the Word with genuine, Spirit-wrought faith. This person endures and over time produces and bears the fruits that we've talked about so much up to this point. Notice the fruit is not uniform: some produce thirty-fold, some sixty, and some a hundred. This is the imperfect progression of sanctification we discussed previously. Though the quantity of fruit varies, the presence of fruit is certain. The true seed, planted in the good ground of a regenerated heart, will persevere to the end if it is of God.

This chapter is about an important observation of the ultimate assurance. The mark of the reprobate is that they do not endure to the end. The glorious promise of the Gospel, however, is that the true saint cannot fail to endure to the end. You do not save yourself by enduring. You endure because you are saved. Your perseverance is the final, irrefutable evidence that God has granted you the gift of faith and that He will not let you go. The question is not, "How strong is my grip on Christ?" but, "How strong is Christ's grip on me?" If you look at the Parable of the Sower and see that you are planted on good ground and continuing to draw strength from the Word of God, you have powerful evidence that you are on the road of endurance!

11

The Value of the Scriptures

To this point, we've taken a look at some of the most telling signs and key characteristics to help discern whether a man is in the faith or not by using the Word of God. I don't put much stock in emotions or feelings, because they simply don't change the words or the truth of the Scriptures. It is vital that the Christian understands the significance of the Holy Bible, its inerrancy, its infallibility, and its authority. Our feelings and emotions should be dictated by the Word, not the other way around. I want to take this chapter to explain, to some extent, the value that the Word of God should hold for the Christian.

What is the value of the Scriptures? To the world, it's nothing more than a collection of myths and man-made morals. But to the regenerate believer, they are priceless. Far more valuable than gold and silver. They are the spoken Words of God to His people. I used to say that the acronym for BIBLE was Basic Instruction Before Leaving Earth, but as I have grown, I have come to realize that it's not *basic*, it's not just a *set of instructions*, and it's not only for *before leaving earth*.

The value of the Scriptures cannot be measured as if it were a common commodity. The value of economic commodities like gold, corn, and crude oil, ebb and flow like the waves of the great seas. Their worth depends on the changing markets of man. They could be worth a lot today, and worthless tomorrow. But the

Word of God stands fixed, immutable, and priceless above all else. The Psalmist declared, *"For ever, O LORD, thy word is settled in heaven"* (Psalm 119:89). It is not subject to the opinions of any culture. It doesn't shift and change like the sands of modern philosophy and science. It is a stronghold for all of Gods people. It is the breath of life.

David, *a man after God's own heart*, knew and understood that the value of God's law was far more valuable than any earthly treasure. He wrote in Psalm 19:10, *"More to be desired are they than gold, yea, than much fine gold: sweeter also than honey and the honeycomb."* If you are truly saved, the Bible is not a burden to you. It should be your lifeline. We should see it as the very breath of God exhaled onto the page for the instruction, direction, and conduct of His people, because that is exactly what it is. As we continue to examine ourselves to see whether we are in the faith, we must ask ourselves: Do I value the Word of God? Does my life prove that I hold the Scriptures in the highest regard?

One of the telling marks of a true believer is a desire to be holy. As we discussed in previous chapters, we are not saved *by* our holiness, but we are saved *unto* holiness. This is very important to understand. Again, this process is called sanctification, but how does this process occur? It does not happen through osmosis and it does not happen through mere emotional experiences. It happens through the regular (daily) intake of, immersion in, and conforming to the Word of God.

John's Gospel account recorded the high priestly prayer of Jesus concerning His disciples. He prayed to the Father, asking Him to, *"Sanctify them through thy truth: thy word is truth"* (John 17:17). The entire chapter of John 17 is a prayer spoken by Jesus, and a large portion of that prayer was dedicated to praying for His disciples. I have some good news. It was not just for those present then, but also for us today who would *believe through their word* (John 17:20). He asked the Father in Heaven to sanctify them, and that prayer is just as effective for us today as it was for them then.

What does it mean to sanctify something? Again, it means to set it apart, to make it distinct. It implies being cut off from *the profane* and dedicated to *the divine*. Does this sound familiar? Do you remember from the previous chapters of this book which other word means "set apart" or "distinct?" If you said *Holy*, you're correct! In 1 Peter 1:15-16, he writes, *"But as he which hath called you is holy, so be ye holy in all manner of conversation; Because it is written, Be ye holy; for I am holy."* Peter quotes Leviticus 11, tying the New Testament believer back to the unchanging nature and holiness of God.

Without the Word *of* God, we have no word *from* God. We would have no idea on how to live and conduct ourselves. We cannot grow in sanctification apart from the Scriptures because the Scriptures are one of the tools that the Holy Spirit uses to prune us. *"Wherewithal shall a young man cleanse his way? by taking heed thereto according to thy word"* (Psalm 119:9). Sanctification is the process where God constantly works in the life of the believer over time to remove the power of indwelling sin and allows the believer to grow in grace. The Word has all we need for this task. The Word of God is sufficient concerning all manner of life and godliness! How do we order our lives? How do we order our household? How do we handle our finances? How do we raise our children to be men and women of faith and not heathens of this world? We do not look to the talk shows of the world or the secular psychology of the age. It is all found in the Word of God, the Holy Bible.

Paul instructed Timothy regarding this sufficiency in 2 Timothy 3:16-17, *"All Scripture is given by inspiration of God, and is profitable for doctrine, for reproof, for correction, for instruction in righteousness: That the man of God may be perfect, throughly furnished unto all good works."*

Notice the divine progression in this passage concerning *all Scripture*! It starts with doctrine, which tells us *what is right*. Then it goes to reproof, which tells us where *we are wrong*. Correction simply means that it will tell us *how to get right*, and instruction in righteousness tells us *how to stay right*! Are you searching the Scriptures in prayer and fasting to find His will for your life? Or is God's will just a thought that crosses your mind occasionally? We should all be seeking the will of God for our lives, and His will is revealed in His Word.

Remember the sobering warning Jesus gave in Matthew 7:21, *"Not every one that saith unto me, Lord, Lord, shall enter into the kingdom of heaven; but he that doeth the will of my Father which is in heaven."* Knowing the will of God is of utmost importance, and it is only found when the believer immerses himself in the Word. I heard Justin Peters speaking at a conference in Atlanta once, and he said, "If you want to hear God speak to you, read your Bible. If you want to hear Him speak to you audibly, read it out loud." This is true. So many times, we are waiting for God to speak from the celestial clouds of glory and talk to us like He spoke to Moses through the burning bush. Friends, He has spoken to us. He has spoken to us FULLY and FINALLY through His Son Jesus Christ. The writer of Hebrews wrote, *"God, who at sundry times and in divers manners spake in time past unto the fathers by the prophets, Hath in these last days spoken unto us by his Son..."* (Hebrews 1:1-2a)

But the Scriptures do much more than just tell us how to live. They tell us *who God is*. This is one of the great failings of the modern age church. Sadly, a lot of well-meaning people worship a god of their own imagination, a god crafted in their own image rather than the God of the Bible. By reading and studying the Scriptures, it allows us to actually know the person and character of God instead of relying on someone else to tell us about Him. You *can* know God! He is not some dark, shadowy figure up in the clouds. *"This then is the message which we have heard of him, and declare unto you, that God is light, and in him is no darkness at all"* (1 John 1:5).

He has revealed Himself in His Word. When we open the Bible, we are treading on holy ground. It is where we come face to face with His attributes. By spending time in His Word, you will learn a lot more about the nature and attributes of God than you will if you only attend a church service once a week! Even at a solid, Bible believing, Bible preaching church; there's only so much time you can spend at church learning. You have to take Bible reading and studying and make it a daily habit. The more time you spend in the Word, the more you will learn and be conformed to His image (which may be a lot different than you think it is now).

You will see His holiness, in that He is completely set apart and distinct. He is not like us. *"For my thoughts are not your thoughts, neither are your ways my ways, saith the LORD"* (Isaiah 55:8). You will see His Immutability. In a world that changes its definition of morality and everything else every decade, we serve a God who says in Malachi 3:6, *"For I am the*

LORD, I change not. " If He was, He always will be. If He is, He always was. We have the unbroken link of God's character from the Old Testament to the New Testament. Be sure of this: The God of Genesis is the God of Revelation. Some think the God of the Old Testament is like a "mean old man in the sky", but Jesus in the New Testament is much different in that He is much more kind and gentle... Let's just say, they haven't quite read through the last book of the New Testament yet...

Consider Isaiah and his response to his vision of seeing the Lord. He did not run up to give God a high-five. He pronounced a curse of death on himself: *"Woe is me! for I am undone; because I am a man of unclean lips"* (Isaiah 6:5). We see the same reaction in the New Testament. When Peter realized who Jesus was in Luke 5:8, *"he fell down at Jesus' knees, saying, Depart from me; for I am a sinful man, O Lord."* The true God produces the fear of the Lord and an immediate urge to confess sin. The god of modern imagination produces only casual indifference at best, but mainly just "warm feelings" and excitement.

By living in the Word, you will see His Justice and Wrath. These attributes are rarely spoken of from pulpits and podiums today because they come across as "offensive" to a lot of people. Remember the sons of Aaron, Nadab and Abihu. They were priests and they had clear instruction in Exodus 30:9 regarding incense, yet on their own accord, they offered strange fire before the Lord. They approached God in a way that He had commanded them not to. The result? *"And there went out fire from the LORD, and devoured them, and they died before the LORD"* (Leviticus 10:2).

Remember also Uzzah, who reached out his hand to steady the Ark of God when the ox stumbled. To the human mind, Uzzah was being helpful because he didn't want the Ark to hit the dirt. But God had commanded that the Ark never be touched by human hands (Numbers 4:15). What did God do? Did He yell from Heaven praising Uzzah for his righteous and courageous deeds? No. *"And the anger of the LORD was kindled against Uzza, and he smote him, because he put his hand to the ark: and there he died before God"* (1 Chronicles 13:10).

If we think of these instances as God being unfair and unjust, we must repent of our high view of man and our low view of God. I believe that we are so used to grace being heaped upon our heads that we are offended by the mere thought of true justice. If God were not a forgiving and merciful God, Adam and Eve would have been killed in the garden just as swiftly as those men were. In fact, God was exceedingly gracious to Adam and Eve. The warning was, *"for in the day that thou eatest thereof thou shalt surely die"* (Genesis 2:17). The truth is, they did not die that day (physically). God let them live. The worst curse fell upon the serpent. The serpents end was made final, but man was allowed to continue on in life, though not without toils, labor, and pains. That is mercy. That is mankind not getting what was truly deserved.

You will also see His Love. When you understand His holiness and His wrath against sin, only then can you appreciate His love. You will see that God Himself *is love* (1 John 4:8). *"For God so loved the world, that he gave his only begotten Son..."* (John 3:16). You can study the love displayed by God at Calvary for the rest of your life and never comprehend the magnitude of what was done for us that day. Therefore, the value of Scripture for the believer is the privilege of knowing God as He truly is, not as the world wishes Him to be.

The Scriptures are also the believer's only defense against the wolves that ravage the flock. *"My people are destroyed for lack of knowledge"* (Hosea 4:6). This passage has an application as wide as the Pacific Ocean, and just as deep. But for our immediate focus, we'll discuss the implications it has on the value of the Scriptures. If there was ever a period of time when heresy was taught openly in the land, it is in our present age (and it seems to be getting worse since the advent of social media). How will you know if a teacher is false if you, having a copy of Scripture, are never in it? To know what is false, you must first know what is true. Bankers are trained to identify counterfeit money, not by studying the counterfeits, but by studying the real bills so intensely that the moment they touch a fake, they can recognize and reject it.

How do you know for certain that the "Word of Faith" teachers are heretics? How do you know that people like Kenneth Copeland, Joyce Meyer, Joel Osteen, and the rest of the "name it, claim it" crowd are peddling a different gospel? They all have this one thing in common: their followers do not know the Word of God. They rely on a man (or woman) to tell them what God says, rather than searching the Scriptures for themselves. If these "motivational speakers" were to stand before a crowd of people who knew the Bible, those speakers would be out of a job within the hour!

We, on the other hand, should imitate the Bereans. *"These were more noble than those in Thessalonica, in that they received the word with all readiness of mind, and searched the Scriptures daily, whether those things were so"* (Acts 17:11). They didn't even trust the Apostle Paul blindly! They checked his teaching against the holy text and decided for themselves whether he was right or not! The best way, by far, to battle false teachings is to know the true teaching. *"Prove all things; hold fast that which is good"* (1 Thessalonians 5:21).

Lastly, Scripture is the most valuable tool that we have to fight against Satan and his deception. When the Apostle Paul lists the armor of God in Ephesians 6, he lists the helmet of salvation, the breastplate of righteousness, the shield of faith, the loins girt with truth, and feet shod with the Gospel of peace. These are primarily for defense mechanisms. But then, he hands us the weapon, which is *"...the sword of the Spirit, which is the word of God"* (Ephesians 6:17). Look at the example of Jesus in Matthew 4:1-11. Jesus was led into the wilderness to be tempted by the devil. He had fasted forty days and forty nights, so it's safe to assume that He was physically weak, yet remained spiritually unconquerable. Notice how He fought the fight against Satan. He did not use His divine power to subdue Satan, or call legions of angels to take him away. He did not use "feel good" quotes from the philosophers from before His time like Parmenides, Heraclitus, or Plato. No, no. Every time Satan tempted Jesus, the Lord replied with these three words: "It is written."

When Satan tempted Him with the desires of physical things (bread), Jesus quoted Deuteronomy 8:3. When Satan tempted Him to test God, Jesus quoted Deuteronomy 6:16. Even when Satan tried to use Scripture out of context against Him by quoting Psalm 91 (while twisting its meaning), Jesus replied again with Scripture, IN CONTEXT. If the Son of God, the very Word made flesh (John 1:14), relied on the written Word to defeat the enemy, how much more do we need it? And let me add, how much more do we need it IN CONTEXT? *"For the word of God is quick, and powerful, and sharper than any twoedged sword, piercing even to the dividing asunder of soul and spirit, and of the joints and marrow, and is a discerner of the thoughts and intents of the heart"* (Hebrews 4:12).

We have established that the Bible is the source of life, the revelation of God's glory, our shield against error, our sword against the enemy, and many other things. Yet, Bibles gather dust on the shelves of professing Christians all across this land. Consider this simple math exercise: There are 1,189 chapters in the Bible. If you read roughly 3 to 4 chapters a day, you will read the entire Bible in a year. If you read 10 chapters a day, you could read the entire Bible through 3 times per year with 9 days to spare. What would it do for your personal sanctification if you read through the Bible THIRTY TIMES over the next ten years? How much better would you know God? How much more would you hate sin? How much easier would it be to walk in holiness, knowing the precepts of the Lord? Would that be too hard? We often make excuses for our lack of time while we spend hours on social media, watching t.v., or playing around with mind-numbing hobbies while our Bibles sit cold on the shelf.

The lost soul finds the Bible boring, confusing, or offensive. *"But the natural man receiveth not the things of the Spirit of God: for they are foolishness unto him: neither can he know them, because they are spiritually discerned"* (1 Corinthians 2:14). But the saved man? He says with Job, *"I have esteemed the words of his mouth more than my necessary food"* (Job 23:12). Take some time to examine yourself. Do you value the Scriptures? For where your treasure is, there will your heart be also.

12

The Gospel

We have spent many pages examining ourselves. We have looked at the fruit of our lives, the desires of our hearts, and the direction of our walk. My prayer is that as you have read through this short writing, the Holy Spirit has begun to prick your conscience. Maybe you have come to the realization that you have been *"weighed in the balances and found wanting."* (Daniel 5:27) If you have come to the conclusion that you are not saved, or that you are scared at the thought of standing before a Holy God, do not close this book in despair! There is a remedy! To understand the Gospel (which means *Good News*), we first have to understand why we need this good news. Good news is only good to those who understand the reality and gravity of their position. Think about this: What man who thinks himself to be well reaches toward the medicine cabinet? To understand the salvation of man, we don't need to start with man, but with God.

A proper understanding of the Gospel should begin with the nature of the God, not the need of man. We will never understand the need of man until we know who God is! God is not just some high-powered, benevolent grandfather in the sky who keeps a list of our rights and wrongs. That sounds a whole lot like Santa Claus, but nothing like the thrice-holy King of Glory! In Isaiah 6:3, the seraphim cry out one to another, *"Holy, holy, holy, is the LORD of hosts: the whole earth is full of his glory."* To be holy means that God is (as we've discussed multiple times up to this point) utterly distinct. He is morally pure and without blemish.

He is separated from all that is common or unclean. Habakkuk 1:13 says of God: *"Thou art of purer eyes than to behold evil, and canst not look on iniquity."* 1 John 1:5 says that *"God is Light, and in Him is no darkness at all."*

Since God is *Holy*, He is also *Just*. A good judge cannot let a criminal go free. Think about this: If He did, He would be a *corrupt* judge. God is the righteous Judge of all the earth. He has established a law, written them on stone tablets and written them on the hearts of men. His perfect justice demands that every violation of that law be punished. *"He will by no means clear the guilty"* (Exodus 34:7). This presents the greatest dilemma in the universe! How can a perfectly just God forgive wicked men and not be considered a corrupt judge?

This brings me to my next point; you and me. Since God is Holy, what does that mean for us? Make no mistake, the Scriptures do not put sinful man up on the podium of righteousness, but rather under it! They do not tell us that we are *"good people who make mistakes"* as some of the big speakers of our day would have us to believe. The Bible tells us that we are rebels of the highest order committing high treason against King of Glory! When Adam fell in the Garden of Eden, the human race fell with him. At birth, we inherited a nature that is corrupt, twisted, and hostile toward God. Psalm 51:5 says, *"Behold, I was shapen in iniquity; and in sin did my mother conceive me."* Jeremiah 17:9 tells us, *"The heart is deceitful above all things, and desperately wicked: who can know it?"*

According to Psalms 51:5, from the moment of our conception we were alienated from God. You can see this as plain as day if you have ever raised a child. You do not have to teach them to lie, to be selfish, or swing their arms in fits of rage and hit when they get angry. They do it by nature. We sin because we are sinners. Paul paints a devastating picture of our condition in Romans 3:10-12: *"As it is written, There is none righteous, no, not one: There is none that understandeth, there is none that seeketh after God. They are all gone out of the way, they are together become unprofitable; there is none that doeth good, no, not one."* You might try to say that you have done good things, like giving to charity or helping your old neighbor get their groceries inside, but in the eyes of a Holy God, even our so-called "righteous" deeds are stained with the sin of pride and arrogance. Isaiah 64:6 says, *"But we are all as an unclean thing, and all our righteousnesses are as filthy rags."*

The fact is, we are not merely spiritually sick people in need of a spiritual medicine. It's much worse than that. We are spiritually *dead*. Ephesians 2:1 says that, as lost souls, we were *"dead in trespasses and sins."* A dead man simply cannot perform lifesaving surgery on himself. A dead man cannot choose in and of himself to live. He needs a supernatural miracle! So, here we stand as guilty before a Holy God, the Perfect Judge. We are morally bankrupt, unable to pay our debt, and deserving of the eternal wrath of God in a place that the Bible calls Hell. This is the bad news for us. Better stated, this is TERRIBLE news for us! It is the pitch-black backdrop upon which the diamond of the Gospel shines.

But God, in His infinite mercy did not leave us in our ruined and pitiful standing. He did what we could never do. He sent His Son. *"But when the fulness of the time was come, God sent forth his Son, made of a woman, made under the law"* (Galatians 4:4). Jesus Christ is not just a moral teacher. He is not just another prophet. He is the eternal Son of God, the second person of the

Trinity, who took on human flesh. He is truly God, and truly Man. He had to be man to represent us, and He had to be God to save us, for *"Salvation is of the LORD."* (Jonah 2:9) Jesus lived the life that you and I could not live. This is often overlooked, but it is a vital truth. For thirty-three years, Jesus walked this earth and never sinned once. He was tempted in every point just like we are, yet without sin according to Hebrews 4:15. He loved the Lord His God with all His heart, soul, mind, and strength for every second of every day, without fail. He fulfilled every point of the law of God perfectly.

We now come to the heart of the Gospel; the cross. Why did Jesus die? It was not merely an example of love. It was not a random circumstance where things somehow got out of hand and Rome ended up "winning the day." It was a divine appointment orchestrated from eternity past to accomplish His will for His people. On the cross, there was a great exchange that took place. The greatest exchange. God the Father took all of the sins of His people; all their lies, lusts, thefts, blasphemies, hatred... He took them all and laid them upon His Son, Jesus Christ. Isaiah 53:6 says, *"All we like sheep have gone astray; we have turned every one to his own way; and the LORD hath laid on him the iniquity of us all."*

You can dwell on this for the rest of your days and never fully grasp what was done on our behalf. But it wasn't just that He carried our iniquity and transgressions. He also took our punishment. The wrath of God that was stored up for me and for you! The cup that we deserved to drink for all eternity was poured out on the Son of God at Calvary! The Bible calls this act of substitution *propitiation. "Herein is love, not that we loved God, but that he loved us, and sent his Son to be the propitiation for our sins"* (1 John 4:10) Also, *"Whom God hath set forth to be a propitiation through faith in his blood..."* (Romans 3:25) To be a "propitiation" means to be a substitutionary sacrifice that satisfies wrath. On the cross, Jesus satisfied the Holy Justice demanded by God. He paid the sin-debt in full! That is why His final words were *"It is finished"* (John 19:30). The great transaction was complete. The justice of God fell upon the Substitute so that mercy could be poured out upon the sinner. Two major things happened on the cross, and it's referred to as "double imputation". Not only did God take the punishment from us and leave us *neutral*, but He also imputed to us the righteousness of Christ. 2 Corinthians 5:21 explains this double imputation, *"For he hath made him to be sin for us, who knew no sin; that we might be made the righteousness of God in him."* He took our filthy rags, and He gave us His robe of righteousness.

They buried Jesus in a borrowed tomb, but the grave could not hold Him! On the third day, Jesus Christ rose from the dead. If Jesus had stayed in the tomb, we would still be in our sins. But because He lives, we know that death has been conquered! *"Who was delivered for our offences, and was raised again for our justification"* (Romans 4:25). The Christian can now face death without fear of eternal consequences! *"O death, where is thy sting? O grave, where is thy victory?"* (1 Corinthians 15:55) He ascended into Heaven according to the Scriptures and is now seated at the right hand of the Father. He is now our High Priest. He is the great Mediator who pleads His blood for His people! *"Wherefore he is able also to save them to the uttermost that come unto God by him, seeing he ever liveth to make intercession for them"* (Hebrews 7:25).

You may be wondering how this salvation becomes yours? Remember from the early chapters of this book that most other religions say "do", but The Gospel of Jesus Christ says "Done!" Other religions give you a to-do list. Pray five times a day, give money, stop cussing, be a good person, and *maybe* God will accept you. But remember, your righteousness is as filthy rags, and you cannot bribe the omniscient Judge! The Bible teaches that salvation is a free gift, received by faith alone. Ephesians 2:8-9 makes this abundantly clear, *"For by grace are ye saved through faith; and that not of yourselves: it is the gift of God: Not of works, lest any man should boast."*

As I have stated multiple times in this writing, in Christianity, you do not work *for* your salvation. You work *from* your salvation. You cannot earn it by performing any manner of outward work. You cannot perform a list of duties that will make you clean and acceptable to God. The blood of bulls and goats could not take away sin, and neither can your tears of remorse or your church attendance. Only the Blood of Jesus Christ cleanses us from all sin (1 John 1:7).

I want to speak to the heart that is fearful of standing before a Holy God. Do you feel that you are too broken to come to Christ? Do you feel that you have sinned too much, or that you are too weak to maintain a Christian walk? Then you need to know the heart of the Savior. He said in Matthew 11:28-30, *"Come unto me, all ye that labour and are heavy laden, and I will give you rest. Take my yoke upon you, and learn of me; for I am meek and lowly in heart: and ye shall find rest unto your souls. For my yoke is easy, and my burden is light."*

He is graceful, merciful, and He is approachable. Furthermore, He knows that you are weak, and He knows that you are frail.

Psalm 103:14 gives us tender assurance that *"he knoweth our frame; he remembereth that we are dust."* Jesus lived in human flesh, so He knows what it is to be tired, and what it is to be hungry, and what it is to be grieved. He knows what it is to live in a sin-cursed world. He is not asking you to "clean up your life" before you come to Him. He is telling you to come to Him so that He can wash you clean. In Christ, you are safe from the wrath of God, safe from the tyranny of Satan, and safe from the eternal penalty of sin. He offers you an *"inheritance incorruptible, and undefiled, and that fadeth not away, reserved in heaven for you"* (1 Peter 1:4).

Dear reader, I want to appeal back to the overarching theme of this book and ask: "Are you saved?" If the Holy Spirit has opened your eyes to your sin and awakened your conscience to show you your need for a Savior, there is only one response required of you: Repentance and Faith! Jesus began His ministry with these words: *"The time is fulfilled, and the kingdom of God is at hand: repent ye, and believe the Gospel"* (Mark 1:15). Reflect again on the earlier chapter of repentance. Remember that repentance is not just crying and feeling bad over the consequences of your sin. Repentance is a change of mind that leads to a change of direction. It is agreeing with God that you are wrong and He is right. It is turning your back on your sin and self-righteousness while turning toward Christ. It is a surrender. It is saying, "I no longer want to be the lord of my life."

Reflect also on the first chapter about faith. Remember that faith is not just believing facts about Jesus. The devil knows the facts about Jesus, and he trembles (James 2:19). Saving faith is *trust*. Imagine you are on a cliff, and the edge crumbles. You are hanging by a root, dangling over a pit. Jesus Christ stands on the solid rock and extends His hand. Faith is not looking at His hand and calculating if it is strong enough. Faith is not trying to pull yourself up by your own strength. Faith is letting go of what you have and grabbing hold of His hand. It is falling upon Christ and saying "Lord, be merciful to me, a sinner. If You do not save me, I cannot be saved."

Romans 10:9 promises *"That if thou shalt confess with thy mouth the Lord Jesus, and shalt believe in thine heart that God hath raised him from the dead, thou shalt be saved."* Romans 10:13 seals it by stating, *"For whosoever shall call upon the name of the Lord shall be saved."* There is no magical prayer to recite or alms to give. God looks at the heart. If you see your need, run to Him. Go to Him in the quiet of your heart and confess to Him your filthiness. Acknowledge His holiness, thank Him for the cross, and finally trust in His finished work. Cast yourself upon the mercy of the Judge, and you will find that He is also a tender and comforting Father. Run to the Him and find rest! *"He that believeth on the Son hath everlasting life: and he that believeth not the Son shall not see life; but the wrath of God abideth on him"* (John 3:36).

May God bless His people. Soli Deo Gloria

www.ingramcontent.com/pod-product-compliance
Lightning Source LLC
Chambersburg PA
CBHW020759130626
46554CB00006B/2262